The War of th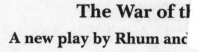

A new play by Rhum and

methuen | drama
LONDON • NEW YORK • OXFORD • NEW DELHI • SYDNEY

METHUEN DRAMA
Bloomsbury Publishing Plc
50 Bedford Square, London, WC1B 3DP, UK
1385 Broadway, New York, NY 10018, USA
29 Earlsfort Terrace, Dublin 2, Ireland

BLOOMSBURY, METHUEN DRAMA and the Methuen
Drama logo are trademarks of Bloomsbury Publishing Plc

First published in Great Britain by Methuen Drama 2021

Cover design: Tjaša Krivec
Cover image: Rebecca Pitt Creative Ltd

A catalogue record for this book is available from the British Library.

A catalog record for this book is available from the Library of Congress.

ISBN: PB: 978-1-3502-6993-4
ePDF: 978-1-3502-6994-1
eBook: 978-1-3502-6995-8

Series: Modern Plays

Typeset by Mark Heslington Ltd, Scarborough, North Yorkshire
Printed and bound in Great Britain

To find out more about our authors and books visit
www.bloomsbury.com and sign up for our newsletters.

A co-production with Brighton Festival and HOME.
Originally commissioned by New Diorama Theatre

A new play by Rhum and Clay and Isley Lynn

First performed at New Diorama Theatre, London on
8 January 2019

Writer: Isley Lynn

The Devising Company: Mona Goodwin, Julian Spooner,
Amalia Vitale and Matt Wells

Additional Material: Gina Isaacs and Jess Mabel Jones

Co-Directors: Hamish MacDougall and Julian Spooner

Movement Director: Matt Wells

Set and Costume Designer: Bethany Wells

Co-Lighting Designers: Nick Flintoff and Pete Maxey

Sound Designer: Benjamin Grant

Video Designer: Iain Syme

Stage Manager: Lucy Adams (New Diorama and Edinburgh)

Deputy Stage Manager: Carys Davies (tour)

Technical Stage Manager: Paul Milford (tour)

Producers: Hannah Tookey (New Diorama and Edinburgh)
and Sally Cowling (tour)

Executive Producer: Sally Cowling

Image Design: Rebecca Pitt

**Rhum and Clay Theatre Company is led by Co-Artistic
Directors Julian Spooner and Matt Wells and Executive
Producer Sally Cowling**

www.rhumandclay.com

BIOGRAPHIES

Lucy Adams – Stage Manager

Lucy is a London-based lighting designer working in devised work and new writing. She's an associate artist with ThisEgg, having designed *Goggles*, *Me and My Bee*, *UNCONDITIONAL* and *dressed* (Fringe First Award winner) for the company. She's also worked with BREACH Theatre on *It's True, It's True, It's True* (Fringe First Award winner), Poltergeist Theatre on *Art Heist* (Edinburgh Fringe and New Diorama Theatre), YESYESNONO on *The Accident Did Not Take Place* (Edinburgh Fringe) and *[insert slogan here]* (Edinburgh Fringe), Willy Hudson on *Bottom* (Edinburgh Fringe and Soho Theatre), Haley McGee on *Ex-Boyfriend Yard Sale* (Camden People's Theatre) and Paula Varjack on *Cult of K*nzo* (UK tour). Her lighting design for new writing includes *Skin a Cat* by Isley Lynn directed by Blythe Stewart (UK tour), *One Jewish Boy* by Stephen Laughton directed by Sarah Meadows (Old Red Lion Theatre), *A Hundred Words for Snow* by Tatty Hennessy directed by Lucy Atkinson (VAULT Festival and Trafalgar Studios), *The Amber Trap* by Tabitha Mortiboy directed by Hannah Hauer-King (Theatre503) and *The Last Noël* by Chris Bush directed by Jonathan Humphreys (Old Fire Station, Oxford).

Sally Cowling – Executive Producer

Sally is a producer, programmer and consultant. In addition to leading Rhum and Clay alongside Julian Spooner and Matt Wells, she works with a number of arts organisations including the Brighton Festival as its Artistic Associate and International Programmer, curating the international dance, theatre and cross-artform programme and producing the Festival's commissioned work. Sally is the International Associate for Wiltshire Creative: the organisation encompassing Salisbury Arts Centre, Playhouse and International Festival, for whom she leads on international strategy and programming. She also works as a producer of large-scale international projects, including for the 2012 London Olympics.

Until 2010 Sally was the global Director of Drama and Dance at the British Council, creating and managing over 200 theatre and dance events around the world each year. She sits on a number of advisory and award panels, including as an advisor for National Theatre of Scotland, and was appointed an MBE in 2005.

Nick Flintoff – Co-Lighting Designer

Nick trained at the Royal Academy of Dramatic Art and studied documentary film at Met Film School. He ran the technical department at the Gantry, before working for Imagination Ltd as production manager. He then joined their lighting design team working on various large-scale projects. Leaving the corporate world, Nick returned to theatre, where he worked at the Corn Exchange, Newbury alongside lighting many national tours and various shows for the Watermill Theatre. He is currently the Technical Associate for the National Theatre's New Work Department. Nick designed the lighting for Rhum and Clay's *Hardboiled* and is thrilled to be back with the team for *The War of the Worlds*. Nick is a member of the Association of Lighting Designers.

Mona Goodwin – Actor

Theatre includes: *The Visit* (National Theatre), *Misfits* (Queen's Theatre), *Napoli Brooklyn* (Park Theatre), *Blue Heart* (Orange Tree Theatre), *Where Have I Been All My Life* (New Vic Theatre), *Cling to Me Like Ivy* (Birmingham Rep) and *Spring Awakening* (Lyric Hammersmith/West End).

TV includes: Gina in the *Black Mirror* episode 'The Entire History of You' (Channel 4), Rohinka in the mini-series *Capital* (BBC), Elaine in feature-length drama *Marvellous*

(BBC) and PC Tanya Lapham in *Doctors* (BBC). Film includes: *Ali and Ava* and *Freefall* (BBC Film) and *Brighton Rock* (Kudos).

Benjamin Grant – Sound Designer

Benjamin studied at Royal Central School of Speech and Drama and has experience designing for theatre, dance and installation, specialising in devised work and new writing. Recent sound design credits include *Death of England* (National Theatre), *Maggot Moon* (Unicorn Theatre), *I'll Take You to Mrs Cole* (Pleasance Beyond), *Education, Education, Education* (Trafalgar Studios), *Prurience* (Southbank Centre/ Guggenheim Museum, NYC) and *The Road Awaits Us* (Sadler's Wells). Other credits include associate sound designer for *Beware of Pity* (Schaubühne) and associate sound designer for *The Kid Stays in the Picture* (Royal Court). Benjamin is an Associate Artist of The Wardrobe Ensemble.

Gina Isaac – Actor

Gina trained at the Royal Central School of Speech and Drama. Theatre work includes: *A Kind of Alaska* (Rapture Theatre), *A Streetcar Named Desire* (Rapture Theatre), *Made in India* (Tamasha/Soho Theatre), *The Curious Incident of the Dog in the Night-Time* (National Theatre Productions), *Saturday Night and Sunday Morning*, *Top Girls*, *Roots*, *Absent Friends*, *Under Milk Wood*, *A View from the Bridge*, *The Lover*, *Romeo and Juliet*, *David Copperfield*, *Accidental Death of an Anarchist*, *Julius Caesar*, *Two*, *Twelfth Night*, *Road*, *To Kill a Mockingbird*, *All My Sons*, *Three Sisters* and *The White Devil* (Mercury Theatre), *The Butterfly Lion* (Bill Kenwright Productions), *The Grapes of Wrath* (Chichester Festival Theatre), *Lifesavers* and *Photos of Religion* (Theatre503), *Hysteria* (Octagon Theatre, Bolton), *The Winter's Tale* (Salisbury Playhouse), Small Miracle (Tricycle Theatre), *Mother Courage and her Children* (English Touring Theatre), *Belly* (Old Red Lion Theatre), *A Midsummer Night's Dream* and *Richard III* (Stafford

Shakespeare Festival) and *Trojan Women* (Teatro Koreja, Lecce). Television includes: *EastEnders*, *Holby City*, *Casualty*, *The Queen's Lover* (BBC), *Derek* (Derek Productions), *Men Only* (Channel 4), *Pretending to be Judith* (International), *The Bill* (ITV) and *Perfect Disasters* (Impossible Pictures). Film and radio includes: *Beyond* (Big View Media), *Fast Girls* (Unstoppable Entertainment), *Unidentified* (Big View Media), *Walking with Shadows* (Ghost Productions), *The Father Gilbert Mysteries* (Focus on the Family) and *Anna* (Frequency Theatre).

Isley Lynn – Writer

Previous works include: *A Good Story (Canace) – 15 Heroines* (Jermyn Street Theatre, 2020), *Tiny Dancers* (National Youth Theatre, 2020), *Skin a Cat* (national tour, 2018/winner: Pick of the Year – VAULT Festival/nominated: Most Promising New Playwright and Best New Play in Off West End Theatre Awards – The Bunker, 2016), *Albatross* (NEW – Paines Plough & RWCMD, Bute Theatre and Gate Theatre, 2018), *The Swell* (HighTide First Commissions play reading, 2018), *Totty* (Come to Where I'm From: London – Park Theatre, 2015), *Sie Und Wir* (Werk X, Vienna, 2016), *Tether* (Underbelly, Edinburgh Fringe Festival, 2015), *What's So Special* (The Get Out – Royal Court Jerwood Theatre Upstairs, 2014), *Bright Nights* (Script6 Winner – The Space, 2014), *Sleight of Hand* (Little Stitches – Theatre503, Arcola Theatre and Gate Theatre, 2014) and *Lomography* (Soho Young Writers Award, 2012 – Special Commendation).

Jess Mabel Jones – Actor

Jess is a multidisciplinary artist, producer and collaborator who makes work that strives to incite change. She is co-creator of Total Theatre Award-winning *Backstage in Biscuit Land* with Touretteshero, *The Paper Man* with Improbable and Total Theatre Award-shortlisted *The Flop* with Hijinx and Spymonkey. Jess is co-founder of the inclusive punk collective Where's My Vagina? who create disruptive happenings and digital artworks, and is one half of creative partnership Motherhoody, which makes radical public interventions through workshops and film. Jess is neurodivergent and an alumna of Rose Bruford and The BRIT School. *www.jessmabeljones.com*

Hamish MacDougall – Co-Director

Hamish is a theatre maker and works primarily as a director, performer and dramaturg. His work derives from a devised, collaborative process and he has worked with theatre companies, comedians and performance artists. Hamish is also an Associate Artist with Kandinsky Theatre Company.

Shows Hamish has worked on have been presented at venues such as New Diorama Theatre, Soho Theatre, Southbank Centre, Schaubühne and Battersea Arts Centre as well as national and international tours. Awards and nominations include an Off West End Theatre Award for Best Ensemble, the Pleasance Best Comedy Show Award, the Brighton Fringe Comedy Award and a nomination for the Edinburgh Comedy Award. The show *Soothing Sounds for Baby* which Hamish directed was listed in the *Guardian*'s top ten shows of the year (across all art forms) in 2015.

Pete Maxey – Co-Lighting Designer

Pete is a lighting designer and production stage manager with a wealth of experience in theatre and dance. After training at Middlesex University he spent two years with the National Theatre's New Work department, assisting the development of new productions including *Anna*, *Treasure Island*, *Everyman* and *The Elephantom*. He later joined the technical team at Sadler's Wells, the UK's premier dance theatre, and now works with UK and international companies, making and touring shows around the world. Pete also runs technical theatre workshops for the National Theatre and local schools.

As lighting designer: *Nutcracker* (Ballet Central, ADC Theatre), *Salomé* (Cockpit Theatre and UK tour), *Bromley Bedlam Bethlehem* (Old Red Lion Theatre), *Bon Ami* (VAULT Festival, 2019), *The War of the Worlds* (Edinburgh Festival Fringe 2019 and UK/International tour 2020), Breakin' Convention Festival 2017/18/19 (Sadler's Wells), *Wild Card: Spoken Movement* (Sadler's Wells), *The Girl Who Never Looked Up* (National Theatre), *Other [Please Specify]* (Platform Islington), *The Wolves of Willoughby Chase* (Watermill Theatre), *Twelfth Night* (Watermill Theatre), *Dying For It* (Brockley Jack Theatre) and *Ten Women* (Ovalhouse).

Julian Spooner – Co-Director and Actor

Julian is an award-winning actor, director and writer. Having gained a BA in Drama at the University of Bristol, he went on to study at École Jacques Lecoq for two years, where he co-founded Rhum and Clay Theatre Company, for which he is Co-Artistic Director. He has co-created and performed in all of Rhum and Clay's productions. In 2018 he won The Stage Award for Acting Excellence for his acclaimed performance in the solo show *Mistero Buffo* (Arcola Theatre/Underbelly), directed Rhum and Clay's hit show *Testosterone* (UK and international tours), and co-directed and performed in *64 Squares*. He is also a writer and director for film, producing under Skym Bay Films. His short film *Toby*, made with director Tom Savage, has won numerous best comedy awards at festivals worldwide. He was most recently seen on stage playing Hugh Hughes's father Daniel Hughes in Hoipolloi's *The Ladder* (Adelaide Fringe/Norfolk and Norwich Festival).

Iain Syme – Video Designer

Iain trained at the Royal Central School of Speech and Drama. His work and designs have been described as 'ingenious' by the *Guardian* and 'responsible for bringing shows to life' by *A Younger Theatre*. In 2015 he won the

Association of Lighting Designers Excellence in Video Design award. Iain has collaborated with a range of companies, directors and venues including the National Gallery, BBC, Complicité, Belarus Free Theatre, Katie Mitchell, Two Door Cinema Club and Blur.

Hannah Tookey – Producer

Hannah is an independent film, theatre and audio producer and WCMT Fellow, focused on projects and campaigns about contemporary social and political issues. Theatre includes: DARE Festival (Upstart Theatre, Shoreditch Town Hall), *Routes* (Theatre Témoin, Without Walls and Bedford Creative Arts, UK tour), Change of Art Festival (Amnesty International and Change of Art), *Ad Libido* (Voxie, VAULT Festival, Pleasance Edinburgh Fringe), *All the Little Lights* (Fifth Word, UK tour), *Angry* (Tramp, Southwark Playhouse), *Dry Land* (Damsel Productions, Jermyn Street Theatre) and *Custody* (Faith Drama Productions, Ovalhouse). Film includes: *Pointe Black* (Choreo Arts and This Little Rock, Nowness Premiere), Vimeo Staff Pick *Wargames* (BFI and Film London) and *ill, actually* (BFI and BBC Four, Underwire Festival Producing Award Nomination). Audio includes: *Two by Two* (BBC). *www.hannaheugenie.com*

Amalia Vitale – Actor

Theatre includes: *The Strange Tale of Charlie Chaplin and Stan Laurel* (Told by an Idiot), *Beginners* (Unicorn Theatre), *The Lion, the Witch and the Wardrobe* (Leeds Playhouse), *Primetime* (Royal Court), *The Light Princess* (Tobacco Factory) and *Hysteria* (Theatre Royal Bath). TV credits include: *Trying* (Apple TV), *Midsomer Murders* and *Endeavour* (ITV), *Casualty* (BBC). Feature films include: the voice of Lu-la in Oscar-nominated *A Shaun the Sheep Movie: Farmageddon*. Amalia co-runs All in Theatre.

Bethany Wells – Set and Costume Designer

Trained in architecture, Bethany is a performance designer working across dance, theatre and installation, with a particular interest in site-specific and devised performance. She is an Associate Artist with Middle Child, Hull. Recent work includes: *Rallying Cry* (Battersea Arts Centre), *Busking It* (High Tide), *Distance* (Park Theatre), *A New and Better You* (Yard Theatre), *Legacy* (York Theatre Royal), *Trust* (Gate Theatre), *Party Skills for the End of the World* (Nigel Barrett and Louise Mari, MIF), *The Department of Distractions* (Third Angel), *All We Ever Wanted Was Everything* (Middle Child), *Cosmic Scallies* (Graeae and Royal Exchange), *We Were Told There Was Dancing* (Royal Exchange Young Company) and *Removal Men* (Yard Theatre). Current work includes: *Us Against Whatever* (Middle Child), *Thank You Very Much* (Claire Cunningham, MIF) and *Storm* (Search Party). An ongoing project, Warmth, is a wood-fired mobile sauna and performance space, commissioned by Compass Live Art. *www.bethanywells.com*

Matt Wells – Movement Director and Actor

Matt is a freelance actor and movement director and has been Co-Artistic Director of Rhum and Clay Theatre Company since joining in 2011 whilst studying at École Jacques Lecoq. Recent credits include co-devising and performing in *Testosterone* (selected in the British Council 2017 Showcase, winner of Best Theatre show at Pleasance 2017, UK and international tours), *64 Squares* (Underbelly, Edinburgh, sell-out show and national tour, 2018), *Hardboiled: The Fall of Sam Shadow* (London transfer to New Diorama Theatre and Watermill Theatre, Newbury), *A Strange Wild Song* (Bedlam, Edinburgh, sell-out show, New Diorama Theatre). Matt has run workshops for the National Theatre and the Old Vic and for the British Council in Brazil, Kazakhstan, Australia and, most recently, Venezuela.

INTRODUCTION

In some respects, this version of *The War of the Worlds* is an adaptation of an adaptation, so perhaps it's best to refer to the original first. H.G. Wells's *The War of the Worlds* was a ground-breaking piece of science fiction when the book was published in 1898, and tells the story of a Martian invasion that begins in the suburbs of the English countryside and engulfs the earth. Orson Welles's 1938 radio adaptation relocates the Martian invasion to the US and used ingenious broadcasting techniques to simulate the sound and feel of a live radio broadcast. The radio was the first piece of technology that allowed listeners to 'experience' a live event without actually being there, and later in life Orson himself was not averse to exaggerating the impact of his broadcast as having fooled its listeners into believing the broadcast was real.

Our own adaptation of *The War of the Worlds* explores the mythology surrounding Orson's 1938 broadcast, but also draws parallels with the fervid social and political climate of 2016, just after the Brexit vote and just before Donald Trump's election victory. The internet has replaced the radio as our provider of information, entertainment and stimulation, but our susceptibility to a good story remains the same. We were fascinated by the idea of making a contemporary 'period piece' that explored the very recent past. We premiered *The War of the Worlds* in early 2019 as more and more was being revealed about the role of misinformation and clickbait in the events of 2016, with even more still to be revealed no doubt.

Like all Rhum and Clay productions, this was a collaborative process that has seen the play and the production develop from its beginnings at the small scale in New Diorama Theatre. It is important to acknowledge the huge contribution of two actors no longer performing in the show but vital members of the original devising company, Mona Goodwin and Amalia Vitale. They helped create the production and were instrumental in the shaping of the characters of Meena and Lawson respectively.

Writer Isley Lynn on adapting *The War of the Worlds*:

I don't actually like adaptations as a rule. I became a writer to tell new stories, not retell old ones. And I'm just more interested in putting on work that will pay living writers over dead ones. So when Jules and Matt came to me about adapting *The War of the Worlds* I was hesitant, but won over by the freedom of the brief they offered, which was not to stage a story that everyone already knows, but to make something fundamentally new. I was enticed by the chance to dissect the act of retelling itself, through a retelling that doesn't play by the rules of retelling.

The old adage 'it doesn't have to be real to be true' is so often invoked by writers, but with this show I wanted to place that deceptively simple idea at the heart of the whole enterprise, stretching it and pulling it and testing it and challenging it and pushing it as far as we could. It was a key to the real world events we were playing within, and a core to the fiction we created to explore the potentially disastrous consequences of such a statement.

This approach was intentional from the start, but perhaps also inevitable, considering how much of our influences were stories shared by people who had heard it from someone else who read it somewhere, etc. Accounts of accounts of accounts which time will never let you trace back with any true reliability. Instead, we embraced the liberation that gave us, channelling it not only into how we treated source material, but also into the modern family story: the real drama of the show which reflects our current times even more directly. After all, throughout the devising process we spent as much time talking about family myths and the inconsistencies within them as we did historical and political events. The story and scenes of the Kavakas family is truthfully where I poured the most of my heart.

The result is an adaptation with its fingers crossed behind its back. Ours is not an adaptation of *The War of the Worlds*, but instead a story about the story of the story of *The War of the Worlds*. And the power of stories. It's stories all the way down.

Co-Artistic Director of Rhum and Clay and Co-Director of *The War of the Worlds* Julian Spooner on the origin of the ideas behind *The War of the Worlds*:

When we began reimagining *The War of the Worlds*, the word that kept coming to mind was *mythology*; the ways in which we weave myths that frame our perceptions of self and national identity.

Being Anglo-American myself, much of my American family has settled about 30 miles north of Grovers Mill, the small township that Orson Welles decided would be the focal point of his Martian invasion. In May 2018, I visited Grovers Mill to investigate the real-life impact of the fake Martian invasion. Perhaps the most joyous discovery was a novelty-filled café dedicated to the Orson Welles broadcast. The staff enthusiastically relayed to me story after story of hysterical reactions to the broadcast. The most notable recollection centred around a family who were so frightened by Orson Welles's broadcast that they fled the family home, only to leave an elderly relative behind, who subsequently wrote them all out of her will. Whether this story is true or not, it has greatly inspired the narrative of our show, as has the café itself. It seems apt that a real place, based on a fictional event, should be further mythologised in our stylised theatre production. The trip to Grovers Mill reminded me of our innate desire to believe in a captivating story, to mythologise the past, and how inseparable reality and fiction can become.

Co-Artistic Director of Rhum and Clay and Movement Director for *The War of the Worlds* Matt Wells on the physical language of *The War of the Worlds*:

The physical language of this piece was developed to reflect the sonic journey of the show. A small chorus of multi-roling actors transitioning in and out of focus like the dial of a radio or the swipe of a smartphone. Devised through improvisation, our aim was to physicalise the listening experience of the audience, be they in the analogue, pre-war era of 1938 or the digital, pre-Trump era of 2016. The truth becomes a slippery tale that shifts and changes with the movements of the chorus of performers.

Co-Director of *The War of the Worlds* Hamish MacDougall on the structure of *The War of the Worlds*:

When considering how everything came together in terms of the creative structure of the show, two major threads come to mind. The common thread that runs through from the original novel, via the Welles radio adaptation and to 2016 and beyond is the notion of a Western society surrounded by perpetual fear. Many people's first reaction to hearing that in 1938 some people may have thought there was an actual alien invasion taking place is to laugh and think, 'How ridiculous!' However, in rehearsals we did an exercise that compared events in 1938 to events in 2016 and we realised as a company that the two decades are not as separated as we think. It's a short leap from a time where the world was surrounded by the threat of global war and everyone was glued to the portal of the radio for vital information, to the current, highly uncertain times where that portal has turned into a screen and, as we know, the information coming from that screen is not always reliable. This was the genesis for the idea of looking at the same family, the Kavakas family, in two different decades, witnessing how the past often reflects the present.

The other thread comes more in the shape of one person. We didn't want to lose the science-fiction element as it is so vital to *The War of the Worlds*. We talked a lot about time travel and were very inspired by the convention of the omnipresent narrator in things like *The Twilight Zone*, or *The*

March of Time, a popular cinema programme in the 1930s
that dramatised the news and had a narrative that is pulled
together by a God-like voice of narration. Then it hit us that
this figure was staring us in the face all along and that figure
was Orson Welles. Welles painted himself as a mercurial
magician of the theatre, screen and radio. This led us to
creating a chorus of Orson Welles. A friend asked me after
the show one night, 'Why are all four of them playing the
same character?' Well, we wanted to play with the idea of a
ghost-like puppet master who controls our show. Four actors
playing the same part gives a magical, theatrical and playful
quality where the character of Orson can appear wherever
and whenever they like. It also felt appropriate as Welles has
a timeless quality in the fact that he was an artistic innovator
well ahead of his time, often not appreciated in the latter
stages of his life but seen now as a major inspiration in the
arts worId. As Orson said himself shortly before he passed
away, 'They'll love me when I'm dead.' I think that Orson
himself would approve of what we have done, hopefully . . .

ACKNOWLEDGEMENTS

Isley would like to thank:

David Byrne and everyone at the New Diorama Utopia. Mona the beloved neighbour and Amalia the daffodil. My writing families: Playdate (SK, CA, DR, PC, VP, SL), Crowther (JB, SH, AW), the Defectors (AG, TW, KJ, RZ), the Bangers (BZ, JC, LR, AV, KB, EW). Geoffrey Stuart, my familiar. Joey, my little alien. And Jonathan Kinnersley, my shark dentist.

Rhum and Clay would like to thank:

Our phenomenal Trustees: Anthony Alderson, Grant Brisland, Nadia Newstead, Sophie Wallis and Sarah Wilson-White. Our great *The War of the Worlds* co-producers, particularly Andrew Comben at Brighton Dome and Festival and Kevin Jamieson and Dave Moutrey at HOME. Our long-standing supporters including Sally Polden and her colleagues at Redbridge Drama Centre, the New Wolsey Theatre and the Newbury Corn Exchange and the inimitable David Byrne and our New Diorama family. Our thanks too to Scott Ramsay, whose idea this middle-scale theatre business was in the first place, China Plate, MAST and of course Arts Council England who have supported our work since 2012. On a personal note, love and thanks to Rachel Cowling, Sophie Cullen, Brenda Hamlet and Hazel Lucy Hirons.

To Howard Koch

The War of the Worlds

*Everything that came over this new magic box, the
radio, was being swallowed . . . anything that
came through that new machine was believed.*
Orson Welles

Notes

. . . *indicates when a character trails off*

– *indicates when a character changes their train of thought without a full stop.*

Words in [square brackets] are unspoken, included only to clarify the meaning of the line.

/ is a point of interruption.

Interrupted lines are still spoken in their entirety.

If a character's line ends with – and then their next line begins with – this indicates that these lines are continuous, and are spoken without pause for any interruptions even though others are speaking.

Some longer chunks of conversation overlap each other significantly, and so are placed beside each other.

Act One

A space which is, for now, a sound studio.

An imposing CBS microphone centre stage.

A 1930s wooden radio, playing as the audience enter.

Announcer   *The Columbia Broadcasting System and its affiliated stations present Orson Welles and the Mercury Theatre on the air in* The War of the Worlds *by H.G. Wells.*

Mercury Theatre musical theme.

Announcer   *Ladies and gentlemen: the director of the Mercury Theatre and star of these broadcasts, Orson Welles . . .*

Sound stops.

Four **Orsons** *enter.*

They approach the microphone together.

Orson   We know now that in the last years of the twentieth century this world was being watched, closely, by intelligences greater than man's and yet as mortal as his own.

Orson   We know now that as human beings busied themselves about their various concerns they were scrutinised and studied,

Orson   Perhaps almost as narrowly as a man with a microscope might scrutinise the transient creatures that swarm and multiply in a drop of water.

Orson   With infinite complacence people went to and fro over the earth about their little affairs, serene in the assurance of their dominion over this small spinning fragment of solar driftwood,

Orson   Which by chance or design man has inherited out of the dark mystery of Time and Space.

Orson   Yet across an immense ethereal gulf, minds that to our minds as ours are to the beasts in the jungle, intellects vast, cool and unsympathetic,

Orson   Regarded this earth with envious eyes and slowly and surely drew their plans against us.

Beat.

Orson (*Sigh.*)   Of course nobody heard my wonderful speech at the beginning.

Orson   Wonderful speech.

Orson   It really was.

Orson   No, most listeners were tuned into a ventriloquist.

Orson   Edgar Bergen.

An **Orson** *turns on the radio – it plays a ventriloquist act.*

Orson   Yes, a ventriloquist, on the radio.

Orson   And by the time the listeners tuned into *my* broadcast everything was out of context.

Orson   They believed that Martians were mercilessly attacking this small, sleepy town in New Jersey.

Orson   They believed that journalists died and the army was deployed.

Orson   They believed it all.

Orson   Oh yes. I've been told many times since that my broadcast turned grown, intelligent men into quivering infants.

Orson   I know what you're thinking: stupid Americans. How could they believe that aliens had invaded the United States of America?

Orson   But that was the power of radio.

Orson   Imagine a time where fact can turn to fiction, and fiction to fact.

Orson   Where at the centre of every home is a portal to the outside world.

Orson   This machine could put Roosevelt in your favourite armchair.

We hear Roosevelt.

Orson   Chamberlain in your kitchen.

We hear Chamberlain.

Orson   Hitler in your living room.

We hear Hitler.

Orson   The Hindenburg Zeppelin in flames over your rooftop.

We hear Herbert Morrison.

Orson   And aliens just outside your door.

A cacophany of sound.

We snap to the sound studio.

One **Orson** *oversees the performances of three actors.*

Announcer   Good evening, ladies and gentlemen. From the Meridian Room in the Park Plaza in New York City, we bring you the music of Ramón Raquello and his orchestra. With a touch of the Spanish, Ramón Raquello leads off with 'La Cumparsita'.

Music.

The actors silently check in with each other, secretly prepare for the next segment, scurrying around the imposing Mr Welles.

Announcer   Ladies and gentlemen, we interrupt our programme of dance music to bring you a special bulletin from the Intercontinental Radio News. The Mount Jennings

Observatory, Chicago, Illinois reports observing several explosions of incandescent gas, occurring at regular intervals on the planet Mars. Due to the unusual nature of this occurrence, we have arranged an interview with noted astronomer Professor Pierson, who will give us his views on the event. We return you until then to the music of Ramón Raquello and his orchestra.

Music.

Announcer   We are now ready to take you to the Princeton Observatory at Princeton where Carl Phillips, our commentator, will interview Professor Richard Pierson, famous astronomer.

Change in background sound.

Phillips   Good evening, ladies and gentlemen. This is Carl Phillips speaking to you from the observatory at Princeton. Professor, may I begin our questions?

(Orson *as*) **Pierson**   At any time, Mr Phillips.

Phillips   Professor, would you please tell our radio audience exactly what you see as you observe the planet Mars through your telescope?

Pierson   Nothing unusual at the moment, Mr Phillips. A red disk swimming in a blue sea. Transverse stripes across the disk. Quite distinct now because Mars happens to be the point nearest the earth . . . In opposition, as we call it.

Phillips   In your opinion, what do these transverse stripes signify, Professor Pierson?

Pierson   Not canals, I can assure you, Mr Phillips, although that's the popular conjecture of those who imagine Mars to be inhabited.

Phillips   Then you're quite convinced as a scientist that living intelligence as we know it does not exist on Mars?

Pierson I'd say the chances against it are a thousand to one.

Phillips And yet how do you account for those gas eruptions occurring on the surface of the planet at regular intervals?

Pierson Mr Phillips, I cannot account for it.

Phillips By the way, Professor, for the benefit of our listeners, how far is Mars from earth?

Pierson Approximately forty million miles.

Phillips Well, that seems a safe enough distance. Thank you, Professor. This is Carl Phillips speaking. We are returning you now to your scheduled programming.

Music.

The actor playing **Phillips** *seeks the approval of* **Orson***, who is uninterested in praising them.*

Instead, he privately wrestles with how to make the work more exciting.

Announcer Ladies and gentlemen, a special announcement from Trenton, New Jersey. It is reported that at 8.50 p.m. a huge, flaming object, believed to be a meteorite, fell on a farm in the neighbourhood of Grovers Mill, New Jersey. The flash in the sky was visible within a radius of several hundred miles and the noise of the impact was heard as far north as Elizabeth.

During the above, **Orson** *has exited the studio, much to the confusion of the actors left to carry on regardless.*

Announcer We have dispatched a special mobile unit to the scene, and will have our commentator, Carl Phillips, give you a word description as soon as he can reach there from Princeton.

Now in the tech box, **Orson** *takes over from the operator – pressing a button which makes a strange light suddenly appear – the actors are in awe, but they continue the best they can.*

Announcer In the meantime, we take you to the Hotel Martinet in Brooklyn, where Bobby Millette and his orchestra are offering a programme of . . . dance . . . music . . .

Music.

Announcer We take you now to Grovers Mill, New Jersey.

The sound studio is gone – **Orson** *is gone too – and the actors are now in Grovers Mill in 1938.*

They slowly approach the light, which has crashed to the ground.

Phillips Ladies and gentlemen, this is Carl Phillips again, at the Wilmuth farm, Grovers Mill, New Jersey. Professor Pierson and myself made the eleven miles from Princeton in ten minutes. The thing, directly in front of me, is half buried in a vast pit. Must have struck with terrific force. Doesn't look very much like a meteor, at least not the meteors I've seen. It looks more like a huge cylinder. While the policemen are pushing the crowd back, here's Mr Wilmuth, owner of the farm here. He may have some interesting facts to add. Mr Wilmuth, would you please tell the radio audience as much as you remember of this rather unusual visitor that dropped in your backyard?

Wilmuth Well . . .

Phillips Step closer, please. Ladies and gentlemen, this is Mr Wilmuth.

Wilmuth Well, I was listenin' to the radio.

Phillips Closer and louder please.

Wilmuth Pardon me!

Phillips Louder, please, and closer.

Wilmuth   Yes, sir – while I was listening to the radio and kinda drowsin', that professor fellow was talkin' about Mars, so I was half dozin' and half . . .

Phillips   Yes, yes, Mr Wilmuth. Then what happened?

Wilmuth   As I was sayin', I was listenin' to the radio kinda halfways . . .

Phillips   Yes, Mr Wilmuth, and then you saw something?

Wilmuth   Not first off. I heard something.

Phillips   And what did you hear?

Wilmuth   A hissing sound. Like like a fourt' of July rocket.

Phillips   Then what?

Wilmuth   Well, I looked out the window and would have swore I was to sleep and dreamin'.

Phillips   Yes?

Wilmuth   I seen a kinda greenish streak and then zingo! Somethin' smacked the ground. Knocked me clear out of my chair!

Phillips   Well, were you frightened, Mr Wilmuth?

Wilmuth   Well, I – I ain't quite sure. I was riled is all.

Phillips   Thank you, Mr Wilmuth. Thank you.

Wilmuth   Want me to tell you some more?

Phillips   No that's quite all right, that's plenty. Ladies and gentlemen, you've just heard Mr Wilmuth, owner of the farm where this thing has fallen. I wish I could convey the atmosphere (*through the radio*) . . . *The background of this* . . . Listen:

A building humming.

Phillips   . . . Do you hear it? It's a curious humming sound that seems to come from inside the object. I'll move the microphone nearer. Can you hear it now? Oh, Professor Pierson!

Pierson   Yes, Mr Phillips?

Phillips   Can you tell us the meaning of that scraping noise inside the thing?

Pierson   Possibly the unequal cooling of its surface.

Phillips   Do you still think it's a meteor, Professor?

Pierson   I don't know what to think.

Phillips   Just a minute! Something's happening! Ladies and gentlemen, this is terrific! This end of the thing is beginning to flake off! The top is beginning to rotate like a screw! The thing must be hollow!

Scrambling Voices   She's movin'! Look, the darn thing's unscrewing!

Keep back, there! Keep back, I tell you!

It's red hot, they'll burn to a cinder!

Keep back there. Keep those idiots back!

Phillips   Ladies and gentlemen, this is the most terrifying thing I have ever witnessed . . . wait a minute! Someone's crawling out of the hollow top. Someone or . . . Something. I can see peering out of that black hole two luminous disks . . . Are they eyes? It might be a face. It might be . . . Good heavens, something's wriggling out of the shadow like a grey snake. Now it's another one, and another. They look like tentacles to me. It's large, large as a bear and it glistens like wet leather. But that face, it . . . ladies and gentlemen, it's indescribable. I can hardly force myself to keep looking at it. The eyes are black and gleam like a serpent. The mouth is V-shaped with saliva dripping from its rimless lips that seem to quiver and pulsate. The thing's raising up. This is the most extraordinary experience. I can't find words . . . I'll pull this microphone with me as I talk. I'll have to stop the description until I can take a new position. Hold on, will you please.

Music as we snap to a couple listening at home on their radio.

They are frozen with fear as they wait for **Phillips** *to return.*

Announcer   *We are bringing you an eyewitness account from Wilmuth farm, Grovers Mill, New Jersey. We now return you to Carl Phillips at Grovers Mill.*

The couple listen, making attempts to comfort each other.

Phillips *returns – but this time we only see his silhouette and hear his voice through the couple's radio:*

Phillips *(through the radio)*   *Ladies and gentlemen. Am I on? Ladies and gentlemen, here I am, back of a stone wall that adjoins Mr Wilmuth's garden. From here I get a sweep of the whole scene. I'll give you every detail as long as I can talk. As long as I can see. More state police have arrived They're drawing up a cordon in front of the pit, about thirty of them. The captain and two policemen advance with something in their hands. I see it now. It's a white handkerchief tied to a pole . . . A flag of truce. If those creatures know what that means, what anything means! Wait! Something's happening! A humped shape is rising out of the pit. I can make out a small beam of light against a mirror. What's that? There's a jet of flame springing from the mirror, and it leaps right at the advancing men. It strikes them head on! Good Lord, they're turning into flames!*

Screams and unearthly shrieks.

Phillips *(through the radio)*   *Now the whole field's caught fire. The woods . . . The barns . . . the gas tanks of automobiles . . . it's spreading everywhere. It's coming this way. About twenty yards to my right . . .*

Crash of microphone . . . then silence.

The couple are dead still.

They look to each other, frozen, as static builds, drowning out the following:

A young boy enters, which breaks their spell.

They scramble to get him and themselves out, shouting and panicking.

They are stopped from exiting by the sound of **Meena** *speaking into a microphone as the static dissolves:*

Meena   Truth – the true or actual state of a matter. Conformity with fact or reality. A verified or indisputable fact. Family – a group of people related by blood or marriage. The descendants of a common ancestor. Hysteria – an uncontrollable outburst of emotion or fear. Yes, I'm doing that annoying thing where the host reads from the dictionary, but I think it's important, because what we're talking about this month muddies these definitions, and defies explanation.

This episode is very close to home – my home in fact. Our story today is Margaret's, who was my neighbour. She was a quiet lady, kept herself to herself, but we lived four doors down from each other for six years, so what started with me helping her with her shopping or when the lift was broken eventually turned into a real friendship. She was sharp. No nonsense. And funny. One day she asked where I got my skirt, and when I told her she muttered, 'I've seen better lampshades.' I really liked her, and it made me so sad that she seemed completely alone in the world. I knew she had a son, I'd seen him around a few times, but when I asked if there was anyone else she just said: 'None, dear. None.'

She passed away in June, and it was at her funeral that I finally met that son of hers, Nick. It was only then I really discovered what a rich life she'd had. And when he told me the story you're about to hear, I was blown away.

I'm Meena Galway. 'Everyone Has a Story'. This one starts in a flat in Ealing, with a letter from America.

Change of sound background.

Nick *has entered, holding a letter.*

Meena   It'll pick you up from here, you don't need to do anything special, just be yourself.

Nick   Oh, ok.

Meena Shall we start?

Nick And this is going to be out, uh in, when do you think it will be, public?

Meena I try to release one a month, I've got to edit and everything around work, but actually I've been in touch with a producer and they work on a few big programmes and they might feature this if they like it.

Nick This story?

Meena One of them, maybe this one, I'd love it to be this one. Fingers crossed they employ me so I can quit and focus on this but, yeah, in the first instance it would be a little guest bit. Nothing huge. Well, to anyone but me. So. No pressure. (*Laughs.*) Just for the listeners, can you introduce yourself and tell them what this is.

Nick Uh, sure, yes, well, I'm Nick Graham. Margaret was my mother, I'm her son. Um, this is a letter I found in her attic while I was cleaning up her place after the funeral.

Meena And you'd not seen it before.

Nick No I hadn't –

Meena And / what is it?

Nick – but I know the story. Sorry, it's a letter from her brother. Edward.

Meena And what's the story?

Nick Well the story basically is that – and they denied everything – but they abandoned her. So she left home, ended up here and I never met them.

Meena Would you mind reading it for me?

Nick Ok. It says: 'My dearest Margaret, my place or no, I can never ever apologise enough for what happened. I just hope that one day you can find it in your heart to forgive Ma and Pop. You may never share an understanding but I hope we can share our lives again, as a family, in time. Your loving brother Edward.'

Change of sound background.

Paolo (*on the phone*)   Yeah it's very sweet. Totally charming. You've got a real knack for ingratiating yourself with your subjects and it gets you some lovely moments.

Meena   Thank you.

Paolo   I just would say that you can go further.

Meena   Mhmm.

Paolo   It's nice they're all quite brief, quite youthful quite millennial that, but I think it's a symptom of this lack of depth I'm talking about – take the unique, which you've got, and make it universal. You can be more editorial too, curatorial – remember you're not just a reporter, you're a storyteller.

Meena   Yeah, yeah . . .

Paolo   You'll get there, your potential is obvious.

Meena   Thanks.

Paolo   If you find something that really has legs then do send it over – something that goes for the jugular, that speaks to a modern audience, that resonates with the now. Something that can sustain a listener for more than eight minutes, something we could feature as a whole guest episode.

Beat.

Meena (*gutted*)   Fuck it.

Beat.

Meena (*resolute*)   Fuck it.

She turns on her recorder.

Meena (*into the recorder*)   Margaret was brought up in New Jersey, a place called Grovers Mill. I'd never been to New Jersey, or the States at all, but because of Trump and Hillary, and now this letter (*beat as she considers*), I knew what I had to do.

Podcast music as **Meena**'s *excitement builds.*

Meena   I didn't have any contacts, just a town and a story, but that was enough for me. I had to go there, now, just a month before this massive election. If nothing else I thought it might bring me closer to her. Little did I know just how far the story would take me.

The actors snap into a cafe scene.

Server   Welcome to War of the World Cafe and Diner how many are in your party.

The sound and the action of the scene pauses.

Meena   Yes, you heard right – a War of the Worlds themed cafe. Why was I at a novelty cafe about alien invasion? And what does that have to do with Margaret? Let me explain.

Change of sound background.

Meena   The War of the Worlds is this story from the 1800s, written by H.G. Wells, and it's basically the first sci-fi book.

H.G. Wells   It was the first time I realised that the Martians might have any other purpose than destruction with defeated humanity.

Meena   It's actually quite good. I mean, there's only one female character who just holds a gun at one point and then gives it back to the man, but otherwise I liked it. It's been adapted into a massive rock opera from the seventies.

An actor dances.

Meena   That's pretty cheesy but pretty amazing, and a Tom Cruise movie.

Tom Cruise   Can you think of a plan that doesn't involve your ten-year-old sister joining the army?

Meena   And most importantly for our story, Orson Welles's radio adaptation from 1938 set in . . . Grovers Mill.

Phillips   Ladies and gentlemen, this is Carl Phillips again, at Wilmuth farm, Grovers Mill, New Jersey.

Meena   Hence the cafe.

We are back in the cafe.

Server   Table for one is it?

Meena   Uh yeah just one please thanks.

Server   Ok sure hold on one sec I'll just clear it up for ya.

Meena   Thanks – they've got a coffee machine that's meant to be a big metal alien I think, and there's memorabilia all over the walls, and an antique radio that's playing the broadcast on repeat, and the servers all have antennae on their heads.

Server   Ok here ya go take a seat, can I get a coffee for ya?

Meena   Uh yes please, do you mind me recording?

Server   No, honey, you go right ahead.

Meena   I'm making a – I'm documenting my, / everything I'm . . .

Server   No problem – coffee coming right up!

Meena   The menu is amazing, they've got crater burgers and Martian mac n cheese and heat ray Sloppy Joe's, which I don't really know what that is, and huge milkshakes that look like a heart attack.

Server   Here ya go, you ready to order?

Meena   I think I'll just stick with this for now.

Server   Are you British?

Meena   Yes.

Server   Wow, cool, hey congratulations on your Brexit.

Meena   Oh I'm . . .

Server   Even better for that socialism healthcare right? More money for it or something?

Meena   I don't know about that to be honest.

Server   Well, it's pretty inspiring.

Boss   This just in – it's somebody's birthday!

Server   Hold on, honey –

Server *screams.*

Servers   WATCH OUT FOR THE HEAT RAY!

Server   I'm Carl Phillips! I'm running away! I'm Carl Phillips! I'm ru – ack! Happy birthday, sweetie. (*Returning to* **Meena**.) Sorry about that. So, why are you visiting our little town?

Meena   That's fine – do you have time to chat?

Server   'Chat'. (*Giggles.*) I'd love to 'chat', yeah. Are you like famous over there or something?

Meena   Oh no, no . . .

Server   I bet you are.

Meena   What do you know about The War of the Worlds? The broadcast?

Server   Only from this place and I don't know – I don't think it's that accurate to be honest, don't tell my boss. But there's a bunch of places you can visit if you're interested. We got the plaque and the observatory, and the water tower they shot at it thinking it was a spaceship I think – I'll make you up a list, hold tight . . .

Meena   The water tower seemed like a good place to start . . .

Change of sound background.

Jeff   Private property!

Meena   Hello?

Jeff   This is private property.

Meena   I don't, oh ok, hi, my name's Meena.

Jeff   Hey, how you doing, this is private property.

Meena   Oh I didn't know.

Jeff   Yeah that's my car and that's my house and this is my yard.

Meena   I understand, I'm sorry, I see now that it's / just that . . .

Jeff   You're here for The War of the Worlds, right?

Meena   Yes! Yes I'm just seeing the tower, that's like, that's so amazing, it does actually look like . . .

Wife   Jeff, what's going on?

Jeff   Yeah we got another one.

Wife   Oh for . . . Can you tell her we're eating.

Jeff   I am! (*To* **Meena**.) We're having eggs.

Meena *takes a moment to resummon her energy after this rejection.*

Meena   . . . The plaque seemed like a good place to start –

Change of sound background.

Meena   – Excuse me?

Jogger   Mm?

Meena   Hi, I'm just visiting I don't really know the area but I was told that this park had a plaque in it?

Jogger   Oh yeah, yeah, it's just over that end, you can't really see it, but it's there – You're talking about War of the Worlds, right?

Meena   This is where the Martians landed, right? The Martian landing site.

Jogger   . . . Sure. It's over there

Meena   Oh my God there it is. It's covered by a bush, yep, The War of the Worlds, Fiftieth Anniversary.

Three **Orsons** *have appeared behind her, approving.*

Meena   There's a flying saucer and a family all gathered round the radio and they're all very . . . very . . . and I guess that's meant to be Orson Welles. I wouldn't say the likeness is fantastic.

The **Orsons** *are perturbed by this.*

Meena   It's . . . (*Sighs.*) Honestly I was expecting . . . I don't know, something a bit more . . . (*To a* **Dog Walker** *and their two noisy, bouncy dogs.*) – Hi, oh – oh my God, um – do you mind if I ask you a few questions?

Dog Walker (*distracted*)   Are you the press or?

Meena   No, no, I'm making a podcast.

Dog Walker   Oooookay – no! leave it!

Meena   About The War of the Worlds.

Dog Walker   Oh God.

Meena   So this is where the Martians would have landed, right?

Dog Walker   It's a fiction soooo . . . I don't know what you're asking really – down, boy.

Meena   Yeah no but what's interesting is that on the night of the broadcast this is where they said that the Martians had landed, here so.

Dog Walker   I guess, I don't know – hey!

Meena   Have you lived here a long time or?

Dog Walker   Yep.

Meena   Ok so, are there any stories that you know about the broadcast?

Dog Walker   No, not really. I have to go. Joey! Roger!

Meena *is left again, dejected.*

Meena   I was starting to feel like I was wasting my time. I'd come all this way, spent all this money and, what was I doing here? I was standing in a park. Alone. Looking at a real commemorative plaque to a fake Martian invasion. Jet lag was starting to kick in. I thought, maybe I should just go back to my hotel . . .

Canvasser   Excuse me, ma'am, can I speak to you about your vote?

Meena   Oh no, sorry, I'm not, I can't vote.

Canvasser   Oh right, ET tourist huh? Alien enthusiast? We get a lot of you.

Meena   I'm not a – I'm actually a podcaster – and I told him about Margaret.

Change of sound background.

Nick   Mum didn't like talking about family as a rule, but uh this was the one thing she was very clear about – it's quite the story; someone did a joke, it was Halloween, and there were aliens.

Meena   Aliens?

Nick   Yeah aliens, her parents thought there was aliens coming and they left her in the house, like I said, they abandoned her.

Meena   Gosh.

Nick   Yeah. So what they did was they left her and they went with her brother, not her. For twenty-four hours or something.

Meena   How old was she?

Nick   Thirteen, fourteen?

Meena   Wow, and they left her for a whole day?

Nick   Yeah.

Meena   Were there mental health issues?

Nick   No, no, not like that because they weren't the only ones, there were other people – it was all across America I think, it was a big thing. Mum kept all these newspaper clippings, I'll try and dig them out for you. It was on the radio and everyone thought there was aliens landing and they didn't come back for at least a day, maybe longer. I don't know. So she left as soon as she could. We were broke growing up, really broke, moved around a lot – she had to work really hard to keep us afloat, while her brother Edward got the business and the house and everything back in the States. But I never blamed her. She didn't want anything to do with them after what they did. Who would.

We are back in the park.

Canvasser   That is wild.

Meena   Yeah.

Canvasser   So what was her name?

Meena   Margaret. Her name was Margaret Graham.

Canvasser   She married?

Meena   She was yeah.

Canvasser   So what was her maiden name?

Meena   Kavakas.

Canvasser   Kavakas! They've got a store in town!

*As the **Canvasser** gives directions **Meena** addresses the audience:*

Meena   I couldn't believe it. If this was them, then . . .

The ting of a store entrance bell.

Ted Kavakas hardware, how can I help you?

Meena Hi, um, my name's Meena.

Ted Hey, Meena, how're you doing?

Meena Hi, great, thanks, I, I don't know where to start really.

Ted Well, what're you working with, wood or?

Meena No, sorry, are you Lawson Kavakas?

Ted You're thinking of my wife. I'm Ted Denton. She's a Denton too technically, she's my wife! But you know, it's a family business, family name.

Meena I don't know how to get into this really but I'm, I'm making a podcast.

Ted A what?

Meena A radio show.

Ted Oh.

Meena Actually, do you mind me recording?

Ted Are you here about the election? Because we already know how we're voting.

Meena No it's, um, about Grovers Mill and about the broadcast.

Ted You seen the cafe?

Meena I just came from there actually.

Ted See the coffee machine?

Meena I did yeah.

Ted I made that coffee machine.

Meena Oh amazing.

Ted Yeah my wife was asking the whole time it took so damn long she was asking, 'You finished in there?'

Lawson   You talking about the coffee machine?

Ted   Yeah she's just come from there, she's doing a radio thing.

Lawson   Oh yeah I kept yelling he took so long to make it, 'You finished in there?'

They laugh.

Meena   Are you the daughter of Edward Kavakas?

Lawson (*pleased*)   Yes I am.

Meena   I'm actually here to talk to you about Margaret?

*Everything suspends for a moment, as **Meena** turns to the audience:*

Meena   They looked at me like I was an alien.

*She turns back to **Ted** and **Lawson**.*

Lawson   What about her?

Ted   Yeah what about her?

Meena   So, the story I'm aware of is that her parents and her brother, / your father . . .

Lawson   You know, listen, they were good people, I don't know, I'm not really sure if we should be talking about this on the the the . . .

Ted   Yeah the . . .

Lawson   Could you turn that off please?

Meena   Yeah, of course, I'll, hold on.

She turns off the recorder – the sonic world changes: no background sound effects, no voice amplification, we have left the recording.

Lawson   Because I don't think we should be talking to you on that thing.

Meena   There.

Ted   Who are you anyway?

Lawson   I don't want to talk about that. Sorry.

Meena   Ok. Um.

Lawson   So if you could leave.

Meena   I was just hoping to, all I really wanted was to . . . because she passed away recently.

Lawson   She died?

Meena   Yes.

Beat.

Lawson   Well that is very sad but we didn't know her, and I think you should go. And it's really none of your business so I think you should go.

Meena   Well, I – I was – I'm her granddaughter.

Static.

Meena, **Ted** *and* **Lawson** *are frozen.*

Orson *addresses his audience.*

Orson   People do the most extraordinary things under pressure. And I'm good at turning the screws.

Atmospheric music.

Orson   In my broadcast.

Orson   My work of art.

Orson   My utter genius.

Orson   The Broadcast that Fooled the Nation.

Orson   There is one moment in particular of which I am very proud of. Carl Phillips has just been blazed to a crisp. We hear his screams, the chaos, the commotion, and then –

Silence.

Orson   Silence.

Orson   Complete silence.

Orson   I, the maverick, kept that deadly silence for far longer than the script called for. My sweet actors looking up at me, terrified at the stretch of time, the producers furious at the dead air – I was committing radio suicide. But I knew it would work.

Orson   It is in that silence that the listener truly believes.

Orson   They hear the crashing of great alien machines in a soundless night.

Orson   They feel the heat of the Martian rays in the distance, though the air is dark and their skin is cool.

Orson   They see smoke billowing in great plumes over Manhattan, when of course there is no smoke at all.

Orson   And not just the Kavakas family.

Orson   But families all across America.

Orson   Their reactions were irrational.

Orson   Their actions absurd.

Orson   The stories outrageous.

Orson   But all of them absolutely true. Let me show you one such story. Come with me to a small, modestly furnished New York apartment.

One **Orson** *crouches beside the radio, becoming* **George Pulse**.

Orson   This is the humble home of George Pulse.

Phillips (*through the radio*)   . . . *it's spreading everywhere. It's coming this way. About twenty yards to my right* . . .

Orson   He has just heard Carl Phillips incinerated by the Martian's terrific heat ray. He has five dollars to his name. What does he do? He takes those five dollars . . . and he runs.

George *runs, almost colliding with three people.*

One   Woah!

Two   Hey!

Three   Watch it!

George *is stopped by a procession of elderly walkers.*

George   Can you move it!

Old Lady   No, we're old

George *lifts the* **Old Lady** *and runs with her.*

Old Lady   Woaw!

Old Man   Hey that's my wife!

Old Lady   Can you take me to my platform?

George *tosses her aside.*

He pushes to the front of the ticket line.

Ticket Seller   Hey you can't push in there.

George   The the cylinder . . . the train . . .

Ticket Seller   Alright, where're you going pal?

George   Uh – east.

Ticket Seller   Well Connecticut leaves in a minute, you'll miss that one . . .

George *slaps his five-dollar bill to the ticket seller and bundles past.*

Ticket Seller (*calling*)   You need a ticket!

George *makes it onto the train, slamming the door behind him.*

Concessions Seller   Cigarettes . . . coffee . . .

George   Why is this damn thing not moving!

Reader   Yeah this guy.

George   No no.

Reader   I'll get you a scotch.

Passenger You're making me very nervous.

Reader You're alright, buddy.

George I am not alright! We're being invaded!

All What?

Orson They fled in swarms!

Orson Derailed dinner parties, telephoned loved ones, flooded into churches.

Orson Confessing sins long since buried.

Orson Families were torn apart.

Orson And brought together.

Radio static.

An elderly couple listen to the radio.

Phillips (*through the radio*)   . . . *It's spreading everywhere. It's coming this way. About twenty yards to my right* . . .

Edna Charlie?

Charlie *cannot answer her.*

Edna *turns the radio to a love song, which breaks the spell over* **Charlie**.

Edna It's ok.

They embrace, then slowly dance.

Radio static.

Orson Even the US Navy.

Orson This always weighed heavy on my conscience.

Orson Called back from shore leave into active duty to fight the Martians.

Orson I do hope they were compensated.

Orson And those sisters. Poor sweet women.

Bernadette   I need something for my sister and I, something to kill the rats in our apartment.

Valerie   What, you don't got nothing?

Bernadette   Ok what about sleeping pills.

Valerie   Yeah, pills!

Bernadette   We'll take all you have.

Orson   Then they had a better idea.

Bernadette   Two more Scotch please!

Valerie   This is a much better idea.

Bernadette   Please!

Valerie   Much better.

Bernadette   And keep 'em coming!

Valerie   I can see your nipples through your shirt.

Bernadette *hiccups.*

Orson   They sent me the tab, to my delight – I paid it gladly.

Orson   Others sent death threats.

Orson   So many death threats.

Orson   To a brilliant young mind whose only crime was possessing a boundless imagination.

Orson   And a finely honed craft.

Orson   And excellent hair.

Orson   But not everyone was upset.

Radio static.

Phillips (*through the radio*)   . . . *it's spreading everywhere. It's coming this way. About twenty yards to my right . . .*

Sue-Ann   Praise be it's happening! I told you it was gonna happen and it is happening! Bob, make the calls and use the code! Callie, get the cans, leave the green box! Tommy, git your pants on! Let's go go go!

Bob   Gary, Gary, it's happening. D-Day 123 / D-Day 123.

Sue-Ann   Ok we have four minutes to get everything packed, that's your shirts your sweaters your outerwear and your intimates, then we have two minutes to disinfect our bodies and half a minute to get in the car.

Callie   I can't find the can opener!

Tommy   I can't find my pants.

Sue-Ann   This is why we practised!

Orson   Don't worry, Tommy finds his pants just fine.

Orson   But what ever happened to George, you ask?

All   What!

George   We're under attack!

Woman   What attack?

What are you talking about?

George   I'm talking about the cylinder that came down – they couldn't explain it, they opened it up and then everything went silent!

Woman   Who said this?

George   The professor – he didn't know what it was, and then there were no more stations!

Orson   George.

George   What!

Orson   Can I show you something.

George   Who are you?

Orson   Have a look at this.

George   What is it –

Orson   Page 12, 8 o'clock, What does it say.

George   Ventriloquist act.

Orson   No, CBS!

George   The War of the . . . Worlds.

Orson   By?

George   Orson Welles.

Train starts to move.

Orson *gives* **George** *a five-dollar bill.*

Orson   Your five dollars, for the ticket. Enjoy Connecticut.

Orson   Of course I reimbursed him also.

Orson   I'm not a monster.

Orson   I'm a magician.

Orson   I can hoodwink a nation.

Orson   I can make you believe.

Orson   I can make history.

Orson   And while I stood on the precipice of the great adventure that this broadcast would earn me.

Orson   Record-breaking, multi-million movie deals, notoriety and fame.

Orson   A young girl stood. Still. In the house she grew up in. Alone, truly alone, for the first time.

Orson   Her family, gone.

Orson   Her home, so quiet.

Orson   Outside the world is ending.

Orson   And inside, hers is too.

Orson   In that same house, almost a century later, they're serving meatloaf.

Change of sound background.

Ted   That was delightful.

Meena   Thank you so much, it was so nice.

Lawson   You're welcome, honey. That's one of our specials, isn't it?

Ted   It is yeah.

Lawson   We have that one every Saturday.

Ted   Every Saturday.

Lawson   Every Saturday.

Meena's *phone rings – she quickly silences it, but not before clocking who is calling (***Nick***).*

Meena   Sorry . . .

Lawson   Oh no take it if you need to.

Meena   No no it's fine.

Lawson   We don't mind, we're modern.

Meena   It's fine / honestly.

Lawson   Honestly.

They both halt at this sort of funny overlap, laughing a little.

Pause.

Ted   So you came all the way from England?

Meena   Yeah from London, I / mean obviously . . .

Lawson   I'd love to go to London!

Ted   She sure would.

Lawson   Love to.

Meena   You should.

Lawson   Oh I wanted to go on my fortieth and then we didn't go and then I wanted to go on my fiftieth and then we didn't go.

Ted   There's a long list.

Lawson   Ted doesn't like planes.

Ted   And it all costs money.

Lawson   Send me over in a coffin.

Jonathan (*from above*)   Mom?

Lawson   Yeah?

Jonathan   Can you turn the internet off and on again?

Lawson   Not now, honey, can you do it yourself?

Ted   Are you eating dinner or what, Jonathan?

Lawson   Come and eat, it's cold. (*To* **Ted**, *reassuring*.) He's coming down.

Ted   He works up there, he watches a lot of, you know.

Lawson   At least we hope it's pornography.

They laugh.

Jonathan *enters and the scene slows for a moment – smoke from his vape billowing around him.*

Meena *looks at him, like a traveller from another world, but he doesn't notice her at all.*

Jonathan   Mom, did we get Mountain Dew or what?

Lawson   No I didn't get Mountain Dew.

Jonathan   Mom I told you to get Mountain Dew.

Lawson   I thought you liked Pepsi.

Jonathan   I don't drink Pepsi anymore.

Lawson   Do you even like Mountain Dew?

Jonathan (*turning*)   I'm telling you, you gotta get a new deal, you're getting screwed. (*Sees* **Meena**.)

Meena   Hi.

Lawson   Well, if you want a new deal can you find one because I don't know what to do with stuff like that.

Jonathan   Hey.

Ted   Your plate's cold, it's in the kitchen.

Jonathan   I already ate.

Lawson *sighs.*

Ted   This is Jonathan.

Meena   I'm Meena.

Lawson   This is a special guest, honey. (*Dramatic beat*) This is your cousin!

Jonathan   What?

Lawson   This is your cousin from England!

Jonathan   When did that happen?

Ted   Can you take a seat please, we've already eaten.

Lawson   Your dad's not happy – I think you should sit down.

Jonathan (*sits*)   Nice to meet you.

Ted   She's your cousin, alright.

Jonathan   Dad.

Ted   Just making it clear.

Lawson   Kind of cousin, removed.

Ted   But still, cousin, so, you know, just, be polite.

Jonathan   I got it, Dad. So I got a cousin, when did we get a cousin?

Lawson   Isn't it amazing?

Ted   Well, that's why she's here – you're doing a pod . . .?

Meena   Podcast.

Ted   Podcast

Jonathan   What, like serial?

Meena   I wish.

Jonathan   How did you find my parents?

Lawson   Incredible.

Meena   I was just telling them the / story about how I.

Jonathan *starts to vape.*

Lawson   / Do you have to do that now?

Ted   Can you not do that in here?

Jonathan   It's not smoking.

Ted   We've had this discussion – you cannot vape at the table.

Lawson   You're hotboxing my dining room.

Jonathan   It's coconut.

Lawson   It smells like my shampoo.

Ted   Can we please.

Lawson   So (*fanning the smell away with a napkin*) I think we are second cousins and you are third cousins, is that how it works, Ted?

Ted   Yeah that's how it works . . .

Lawson   She's my second cousin? Or would she be his second cousin?

Meena   Basically we're related.

Ted   Say while you've been in our town, you heard about what's happening?

Meena   Uh, no, no I haven't.

Ted Well, let me tell you what that's the real story here. They're taking the jobs. All the jobs. Out of New Jersey. And sending them to China. One Chinese company has bought up all the businesses in New Jersey. That aren't independent like we are. And soon there'll be state laws. Saying I can't employ someone unless they have Chinese heritage. You should do a podcast on that.

Jonathan Oh no, Dad. Not this. Stop it now, Dad. It's happening. Mom, you need to stop it now or you won't be able to.

I can't always be the one who stops it.

Lawson Honey, not right now.

No, no, no.

You stop it.

He's already off on it – No, no, I don't think that's true . . .

Could you give her a rest, honey – she's jetlagged. (*To* **Meena**.) You want some dessert, honey?

Meena I'm ok for dessert, thank you.

Lawson Oh no, come on, you have to have this – (*To* **Ted**.) Honey, get me the dish from the fridge.

Ted Ok.

Lawson Would you?

Ted Ok in a second.

Lawson Please.

Ted   In a second.

Meena   So it's actually the broadcast, that's really what I'm interested in.

Ted   Forget the broadcast, ok. That's hiding the real facts here. Because New Jersey has a long history of strings being pulled. And it goes all the way to the top, nobody's telling the story, CNN sure as hell ain't telling it, they're not talking about it because they're all owned by the same people, this is all over – your princess, Princess Diana, because Princess Diana . . .

Jonathan   I'll get it.

What?

You're always saying do more.

Ok well shit, Mom I'm not telepathic. I'm not upset!

Lawson   No!

I wanted your father to get it.

But look, look at your father – it's not about the dessert, it's a way to – Don't get upset, sweety. (*To* **Ted**.) Would you stop this please Ted – Ted – (*Interrupting wherever he has got to.*) Ted!

Ted   Sorry. Sorry. I'm only saying . . . I've said what I said.

Lawson (*to* **Jonathan**)   Can you take your hat off please, you have such nice hair. Did you have dinner? Dessert isn't dinner.

Meena (*to* **Jonathan**)   What do you think about it?

Jonathan (*has taken off his cap*)   Look, around here everyone's crazy about the radio thing. But, I dunno, man.

Lawson   That's better. You have such beautiful hair. You have the same hair.

Meena   But this thing of people really believing that aliens
. . .?

Lawson   You know maybe I'm too full for dessert – (*To* **Ted**.)
Are you still hungry?

Jonathan   Some of that stuff is, like, I dunno, the stuff my
dad's talking about is very, like, I dunno, apparently people
believed it. It's like it's very old school.

Ted   I am old school.

Jonathan   Yeah, well, you know on the forums about now,
it's like another thing. It's like flat earth, you know.

Lawson   He wasn't like this when I met him, honey, I
promise you, a hippie sure, but all these conspiracy theories.

Ted   Gravity is a theory –

Lawson   Here we go.

Ted   – but we all believe that. And all / I'm saying is that
tunnel . . .!

Lawson   Jonny's a writer. He writes about things on his
website.

Meena   Oh yeah? What kind of things?

Jonathan   Like just . . .

Lawson   He used to write the most beautiful stories, didn't
he used to – he gets that from you, that imagination, he
wrote me a story about a daffodil, and the daffodil *was me*.

Jonathan   Like, I dunno, like, I don't know if you're
following what's happening over here.

Meena   The election?

Jonathan   Yeah there's just so much stuff flying around and
like sources and stuff, you can look at this from all sorts of
different angles there's all sorts of competing facts and I
suppose like what I'm interested in is what story do you

believe, you know I look at lots of different sources and, like, draw my own – not mine always but, a sort of opinion.

Meena   That's cool.

Jonathan   Yeah yeah, right now I'm just – I just finished college.

Meena   Oh great.

Ted   He finished. He didn't complete, he finished.

Jonathan   Oh ok you know what, fuck you. (*Leaves.*)

Lawson   / Oh come on now, Jonny.

Ted   What, it's the truth! Am I lying? Did I lie? Two semesters, which I guess / is a long time.

Lawson   Come back, Jonny! Jonny!

Ted   Let him go.

Lawson   You've upset him now. (*To* **Meena**, *mouthing.*) Sorry.

Meena (*mouthing*)   It's fine.

Lawson   Do you want to stay on the couch? You can't go out in this. How long are you here for? It's a pull-out.

She shows **Meena** *to the spare room with a step.*

Lawson   And there are extra blankets in the chest, ok?

Meena   Thank you.

Lawson   Honestly, it's no trouble, you stay as long / as you like –

Meena   Oh no really . . .

Lawson   What's ours is . . . well. Isn't it.

Meena *and* **Lawson** *share some small gesture of connection.*

Lawson *exits and* **Meena** *is left alone.*

Meena *takes out her phone and listens to a voicemail:*

Nick   Hi, it's Nick and I'm so sorry it's so late, I hope I haven't woken you up, I hope – your ringing was a different – Look, I'm sorry but I've just been thinking about if she would, if Mum would really . . . want it to be public, she didn't talk about family, she was, like me, she was – and if it's going to be featured as part of something . . . If you could give me a call back I'd appreciate it, just talk through things . . .

Meena *hangs up before the message is finished.*

She pauses, uncomfortable.

She shakes the feeling off.

Meena *(speaking into her podcast mic)*   The Kavakas family – on the surface a normal . . .

I was all alone at the Kavakas household, at night . . .

I was trapped in the Kavakas household . . .!

None of it is quite right.

She looks around herself, around at the room.

Meena   So here I was, in the Kavakas household.

The very same house where Margaret grew up.

Where she was left.

Was this her room?

Where these her . . .

She explores the house, microphone in hand.

Ted *is watching a news channel on the TV: Donald Trump is talking about bringing back jobs.*

Lawson *is playing a candy-crush game on her tablet –* **Meena** *follows the sound to where she is.*

Lawson   Oh yes, come to Mama.

Jonathan *is playing collaborative gaming on his computer and listening to music.*

Jonathan   Go go cover me cover me cover me cover me cover me cover me down down Shit fucking noobs cover me you gotta cover me, who's got a bomb fuck fuck fuck fuck fuck help me help me help me help me help me help me help me help me help me FUCK I'm dead.

Meena *slightly (secretly?) enters* **Jonathan**'s *room.*

Jonathan (*turning to* **Meena**)   What! Oh SHIT, sorry.

Meena   Hi, sorry.

Jonathan   Sorry I thought you were – oh you need a ride?

Meena   No your mum said I could stay over.

Jonathan   Oh yeah ok yeah.

Meena   Just one night.

Jonathan   You flew over for one night?

Meena   No but, I don't want to just, take over.

Jonathan   Ok.

Meena   I hope it's ok if I.

Jonathan   Yeah sure no problem. So . . .?

Meena   I just, um, wanted the wifi password.

Jonathan   Oh yeah no sure it's on the router. Under the stairs by the phone.

Meena   Ok thanks.

Jonathan   Sorry I, at dinner.

Meena   No don't worry.

Jonathan   It's just my parents you know, like your parents are your parents and, you know.

Meena   I do yeah.

Jonathan   And like I'm only here temporarily and it's, like, I'm moving out soon, as soon as, you know, go back and finish my journalism major but, like, in my own way you know.

Meena   I did media at uni.

Jonathan   Oh yeah really?

Meena   Yeah.

Jonathan   That's cool. So yeah I'm just doing my own thing right now on the internet and, like, I can do that from here, but, like, I can't do that forever.

Meena   Of course. Well, don't let me interrupt you.

Jonathan   No, no interruption, just getting some work done, for my site. Sorry Mom wouldn't shut up about it.

Meena   She's obviously very proud.

Jonathan   She doesn't read any of it.

Meena   Really?

Jonathan   Only what I send her, turn on the Parental Controls you know. But uh . . . here, look. I think, like . . . talking about aliens and stuff. So this is, like, this is super, I think you'd . . . I'll show you.

They look at the screen.

Meena   Wow.

Jonathan   Yeah, so. Like, this is my site, this is all my content.

Meena   You're writing it?

Jonathan   Yeah.

Meena   Not hosting?

Jonathan   No it's all – and look, hold on – look at that.

Meena   I'm sorry I don't know what I'm looking at.

Jonathan   That's engagement, right, and then . . . this is by article, this is over time, and I've got it broken down by buzzword.

Meena   This is incredible.

Jonathan   I know, right. People read some crazy shit.

Meena   So how long have you been doing this?

Jonathan   Not that long but like I've already seen a significant return. I do like proper journalism but print journalism RIP, right. This is the fucking future. (*Tiny beat*) What do you think?

Meena   You're just making these things up and publishing them?

Jonathan   And people are eating it up let me tell you. Anything with Hillary, anything with veterans, they love it.

Meena   Engagement, that's people who link it and tweet it right?

Jonathan   It's clicks.

Meena   That's a lot of people clicking.

Jonathan   Well that's actually just a drop in the water of an actual population / really . . .

Meena   And your parents don't know about this?

Jonathan (*smirking*)   Can I?

Jonathan *shows her an article.*

Ted   Agh! I found it – Here honey, 'Workers from uhhhh Hoàng An province to outnumber american workers by 2020' I'll print it out for you.

Lawson (*calling*)   We're outta paper I took it to work.

Jonathan   How about that!

Meena Um, so, ok, so do you feel you're, undermining the press by, with this stuff?

Jonathan (*beat*)   What? It's not – no it's not, I just do it for the revenue, the ads.

Meena Some would say / that's . . .

Jonathan I showed you because I thought you'd – because it's cool. Because it's what you're looking at, right? The broadcast . . . I mean, it's not real.

Meena You're publishing it like it is.

Jonathan You're not that stupid. Sorry but like I know you're not – I'm not making this shit up.

Meena You're saying you believe it?

Jonathan Of course I don't. But I don't choose what I write on my site.

Meena How do you not choose?

Jonathan It's just an algorithm. Basically. I just look at the hits, man. I just see where the hits are and do more of that, that's it.

Meena So you're publishing material that you've said yourself even you don't believe.

Jonathan It's not my job to believe it. It's my job to give these people what they want and guess what they want. They want lizard people! Ok. They want Muslim prayer flags in the White House, they want Benghazi, they want Hillary meeting her paedos at a Pizza Hut! It's just what they want. I'm just giving it to them. I wouldn't give it to them if it didn't pay so goddamn well. My clicks – because my clicks, the engagement I got before and after this, it's like . . . compared to before? I'm fucking BuzzFeed right now. It's not my job to stop giving what people want, it's their job to stop wanting it.

Meena But look where you are!

Jonathan   Ok? New Jersey?

Meena   Grovers Mill, New Jersey. Where people believed crazier than this.

Phillips (*through the radio*)   *It's spreading everywhere – It's coming this way. About twenty yards to my right . . .*

Jonathan   No they didn't!

Meena   They did!

Jonathan   They didn't! And you believing it because you read it somewhere and you already thought Americans are all idiots anyway so it props up your your – it's all bullshit! Ok! The hysteria, the reactions, it was all asswad nonsense to sell papers. You think people really believed, really? We might be from asscrack nowhere but we are not as stupid as you make us out to be all the fucking time. That's the real fucking hoax. And you think people really *believe* the content on my site? It's entertainment! It's stories – last week I wrote a story about a woman who married a tree!

Meena   So you don't think any of this / will affect . . .

Jonathan   Listen, I'm just getting out of my parents' house, ok. Yeah some of them believe it, my dad swallows it because he'll fucking swallow anything, but most of them don't. Most of them, just like the liberals by the way, don't really care if it's true as long as it's ammunition. 'I'd run as a Republican, they're the dumbest voters in the country' – you remember that?

Meena   But he said that.

Jonathan *just laughs.*

Meena   He said that in a *Time* article . . .

Jonathan   Snopes it, man. It's bullshit. Do it now, I'll wait, won't take a fucking second. But you didn't did you. You didn't check. Listen, Trump is the asshole driving their ship right now. And the ship is way more important than – And if you think liberals don't think the same fucking thing then you've really drunk the koolaid. You really have. And your precious mainstreams are all polling a landslide for Hillary anyway so maybe you should chill the fuck out about my little site, ok?

Meena   Could you repeat that?

Jonathan   They're the same people, different suits.

Meena   No but, what you were saying about the ship, could you just explain it?

Jonathan   What, you don't get it? You don't understand?

Meena   Um just if you could, go into it, a bit more detail.

Jonathan   Are you . . . are you recording me?

Meena   What no.

Jonathan   You're recording this?

Meena   No, no, no, I'm just interested.

Jonathan   You can't record me in my home / without my permission.

Meena   I didn't! Jonathan, I wouldn't, I am not recording.

Jonathan (*beat*)   Sorry. (*Beat.*) So uh where can I find you? SoundCloud / or . . .?

Meena   Uh, the site's down actually, I'm changing it but I'm not technically gifted like you.

Jonathan   Well, I can help you if you.

Meena   Oh no I'll sort it sooner or later.

Jonathan (*tiny beat*)   I'd love to see it when it's up.

Meena   Oh yeah we'll keep in touch. Anyway, I'm wiped.

Jonathan   Ok.

Meena *leaves.*

She processes what just happened.

She walks back to her room, she takes her recorder from her pocket.

Meena (*excited, speaking into her recorder, a note to self*)   Ok it's not, it's not a – it's not an episode. It's bigger, it's, it could be ... fuck. No, ok, it's a series. Three parts. Or six. This is ... (*Resetting herself.*) Ok, ok, ok, jugular, legs, ok ...

Orsons *have begun to loom around* **Meena**.

Meena (*recording the podcast*)   I'd come here for Margaret's story, and ended up finding a family built on secrets. Built on lies. It felt like I was just getting started unravelling them. I had to stay. I had to get to the bottom of this – of Margaret, of Jonathan, of all of them. What else were they hiding?

Interval.

(*If there is no interval, cut from here to the marker in Act Two.*)

Act Two

Four Orsons.

Orsons   Welcome back, everyone.

Orson   Welcome back.

Orson   To the second half.

Orson   Thank you for, indeed, coming back.

Orson   I think most of you have.

Orson   I hope you enjoyed your drinks.

Orson   Lovely.

Orson   Snacks.

Orson   Yum.

Orson   Toilet breaks.

Orson   Very important.

Orson   And before we go any further.*

Orson   Yes.

Orson   I would just like to make a brief, heartfelt statement.

Orson   That's right.

Orson   Obviously, this whole affair is very traumatic.

Orson   To me.

Orson   To me.

Orson   To *me*.

Orson   And I really am so deeply regretful at this whole . . . whole . . .

Orson   I'm just very sorry.

---

* If there is no interval, cut from **Meena**'s last line to '**Orson**   Before we go any further.'

Orson   So sorry.

Orson   My intention, of course, was to *move* the listener.

Orson   Of course.

Orson   But the scale to which this has escalated it's it's it's it's.

Orson   It's deeply shocking.

Orson   Not at all expected.

Orson   Or intended.

Orson   No . . .

Orson   It's frankly it's it's it's baffling.

Orson   And something I take very seriously.

Orson   Alien invasion I mean, it's aliens. Aliens. Anyway.

Orson   The consequences of this clearly thrilling and finely executed dramatic work, unintended as they were, and while they do admittedly serve as an unexpected metric for our success, far outreach any possible predictions, by anyone. You understand.

Orson   I mean before this we did Dracula.

Orson   That innocent individuals were so deeply taken in by the effectiveness of our adaptation is, for me.

Orson   Flattering, honestly.

Orson   *And* sincerely troubling.

Orson   Of course.

Orson   And upsetting.

Orson   Very.

Orson   And it has taught me a valuable lesson.

Orson   Mm.

Orson   That the skill within me as a creator is obviously powerful.

Orson   Potent.

Orson   Mightily superior.

Orson   And demands great responsibility in its wielding.

Orson   And I do of course.

Orson   Of course.

Orson   Of course.

Orson   Humbly apologise.

Paolo (*on the phone*)   And he says this on tape?

Meena   Yes I've got it.

Paolo   On tape?

Meena   On tape.

Paolo   Ok . . .

Meena   His parents don't know, his dad reads it but doesn't know it's his own son writing it, and of course they have no idea it's all made up.

Paolo (*beat*)   Ok, wow. This is something.

Meena   Yeah?

Paolo   Very much something.

Meena   Great. Yeah I thought so too.

Paolo   I love the family angle, love the personal and the political, love all that, love that overlap. More of that would be exciting –

Meena   Ok.

Paolo   – because you've got Nick's take on this but I want to know how they feel about their family doing that to

Margaret, you know, his mum. The separation. The *shame*. That's the juice, the jugular, the beating heart, you know?

Meena   The jugular, yes, / that's what I . . .

Paolo   It's that family drama stuff that will really capture an audience before we sucker punch with the kid and the implications of all of that, I mean obviously we need more of that too but with something like this we need to entertain as much as inform, otherwise how else do you keep them coming back for the truth? You get them hooked for their own good.

Meena   So, more family stuff?

Paolo   More of all of it. All of it. More detail. More vulnerability, feelings, a tear or two – a wobble in the throat ideally.

Meena   Ok and I'll send you the link to his website, and I was thinking I'd talk to him about what he's doing and why / and really get his . . .

Paolo   Yeah, great, exciting, and listen, when do you fly back?

Meena   End of the week.

Paolo   That's good. Plenty of time. Take your time. Don't rush anything. You clearly have a rapport with them, they obviously trust you a great deal to let a total stranger into their home, they'll open up to you. But don't scare them off.

Meena   Got it, I won't.

Paolo   Meena, I have to hand it to you – I challenged you. And you went there. I mean you literally went there!

Meena   And if I can get them opening up, I could bring that to you?

Paolo   You should bring that to me and I'll bring it to my higher-ups. Get them onboard. Then we can look at further production.

Meena I'll get it.

Paolo It's good stuff. It's current, with a historical flair, taps into nostalgia, should have a broad audience. If you can get that rich personal detail, we may really have something.

Meena Thank you.

Paolo Remember, beating heart.

Meena *allows herself a celebratory fist pump.*

Lawson Good morning, Meena.

Meena Oh, hello, Lawson, how are you?

Lawson I'm ok – you sleep ok?

Meena Yeah, great, thank you. So comfortable.

Lawson Good.

Meena Are you at the shop today? If you're free / I'd love to . . .

Lawson Um no, I'm not, so we could do something if you wanted, but listen, honey, is your dad ok?

Meena My dad?

Lawson Yeah I messaged him.

Meena (*beat*) You did?

Lawson On the Facebook – found a few Nick Grahams on there but I'm pretty sure the one stood next to the camel is your dad because of the hair.

Meena Oh ok. Uh, yes, / that's . . .

Lawson Just a whim, you know, I was thinking about what you said and it's been so great meeting you that I just tippy typed something and ding! Sent it! Ted said I should check with you but I guess I just couldn't help myself. Is he ok? Is he upset?

Meena Is he –? Why, what has he said?

Lawson   Nothing. That's why I'm worried, cuz you can see he's seen it but he hasn't replied.

Meena *struggles to respond.*

Ted (*entering*)   Morning, Meena.

Meena   Hi, Ted.

Lawson   Anyway I've decided it's a waffle day.

Ted   Ooh.

Meena   Oh no actually / . . .

Lawson   Hush, hush, hush, you have to eat.

Ted   Word of advice: take the food.

Lawson   Take the food!

Meena   I've got – no sorry I'm, I've got to – I'm leaving, flying, tonight actually, so I / should . . .

Lawson   You're not staying the week?

Meena   Uh, yeah, my plans changed, sorry.

Lawson   Oh that's so sad – tonight? / Wow.

Meena   Yeah, work stuff.

Lawson   Just a coffee then, I'll start the machine.

Ted   Finish up the big podcast.

Lawson   Is regular milk ok for your coffee?

Meena   Yes thanks – Yeah that's it / get back, get editing

Lawson   Because everyone likes those hippie milks these days don't they –

Meena   But I can't go without . . .

Lawson   – I don't know if you preferred something fancier . . .

Meena   I just wanted to say goodbye, say thank you, for everything you've done, it's so great I got to meet you.

Lawson   It's such a pleasure, honey, really, and let us know if your dad feels like it – it's ok if he doesn't but we're here you know.

Meena   Thank you, I will, and I just wanted to speak to you and make sure I had all the information from my stay here, which has been incredible, and I just wanted to make a tiny recording, if that's ok? So I'm just turning this on.

She turns on the recorder and holds it between herself and **Ted** *and* **Lawson** *– the recorded world returns, everything heightened.*

Lawson   Oh . . . ok.

Ted   Sure, for your podcast.

Meena   Right just for my notes.

Ted   Make me look good!

Meena   I just wanted to ask some questions before I left – is that ok?

Ted   What do you want us to say?

Meena   I was thinking if we could talk about.

Ted (*for the recorder*)   We're in beautiful Grovers Mill, New Jersey, it's a beautiful morning, America the beautiful as they say, at least until November and / then it's flames sky high.

Lawson   I don't know why you're worried there's / no way he'll win he can't, he's crazy.

Ted   There's a lot going on behind the scenes, take it from me, but one way or the other I'm / saying it's . . .

Lawson   It'll be fine, I think this is a whole ruckus over nothing.

Meena   Sorry, I'm just sorry, if we spoke one at a time that would be.

Ted   Do we need to say who we are?

Meena   Uh yeah, that would be great.

Ted   Ok . . . I'm Ted.

Lawson   And I'm Lawson.

Ted   I'm Ted, the father of this beautiful family.

Lawson   Aw.

Meena   So before I go I need to ask you about Margaret.

Lawson   Ok.

Meena   I understand that it's difficult to talk about.

Lawson   No it's fine.

Beat.

Meena   I just really feel like I need to honour her memory by getting to the truth of what happened to her.

Lawson   Ok. (*Beat*) what do you want us to say about her honey? we never met her. But basically I heard and I don't want you to get upset, honey because this is just what I heard – no disrespect to your grandma but she had a mind of her own, and my dad was really shy like me. I'm shy and um, but she was feisty and kicked up a stink basically. She was tricky. I heard.

Meena   Did your father ever tell you what happened that night?

Lawson   I'm sorry, what do you mean?

Meena   What happened to Margaret on 30 October 1938.

Lawson   What did she tell you?

Meena   We found a letter.

Lawson   Right.

Meena   And the letter seems to corroborate Margaret's story that she was left.

Lawson   Ha! Haha! Oh that's . . . uhuh, ok, go on.

Ted   That's a good one.

Lawson   Keep going. She was left.

Meena   That's what the letter said.

Lawson   Right, ok. Where was she left?

Meena   Well . . .

Lawson   In the bar?

Meena   Why do you say that?

Lawson *just looks away.*

Ted   We don't . . .

Lawson   Wasn't home much, apparently. And young too. So if anyone was doing the leaving it might have been her.

Ted   Honey

Lawson   What! She's got a nerve – she was left? Wow. Ok. Keep going. What else did she tell you.

Meena   A lot of this has come from Nick – my dad . . .

Lawson   Who got it from who? You know? My point.

Meena   But there is this letter, from your father.

Lawson   What does it say?

Meena   It says, it's an apology.

Lawson   Ok, a last-ditch attempt to get her back!

Ted   Last-ditch attempt.

Lawson   They were always reaching out! My dad, God rest him, he was always trying and – nothing! That bitch wouldn't even – even when he begged – I'm sorry but that kind of . . . my dad was very distressed by the absence of his sister. He would have made every effort to try and get her back. Because she just disappeared, vamoosed, nothing, no phone calls no nothing, so yeah.

Meena   I know this is upsetting / . . .

Lawson   You think!

Ted   I think – I think what my beautiful wife is trying to say is that . . .

Lawson (*for the microphone*)   She was a frickin' loon! She thought aliens had appeared, that's how crazy she was and then ran off for a few days! Fourteen! Or thirteen / or something like that, young!

Meena   That's not what I heard, what I heard was that . . .

Lawson   Yeah I don't know what you heard, honey, but you need to check your facts. I thought that's why you were here.

Meena   I am, I'm just letting you know that what I heard was that her parents thought aliens were coming, that they took your father but abandoned Margaret. And now you're saying, it's the reverse?

Lawson   I said what I said, did you hear? That's what happened – did you, are you listening? My dad was upset for years because of what his sister did, that's what I had to deal with. He died four years ago – the last thing he was talking about was his sister.

Lawson *is crying now.*

Ted *tries to comfort her but she's too riled up to receive his embrace.*

He turns to **Meena**, *steering her away slightly.*

Ted   Can I ask a question? Let's say your letter's right. As an example. And the story we knew was a fabrication. Not unheard of. So what?

Meena   So what?

Ted   Yeah, yeah, so what? What's this about?

Meena   It's about the truth.

Ted   The truth? What do you care? Does it matter now? It's done now, we've got to live with it now, that's it.

Meena   I care because someone's life was potentially ruined by the actions of your side of the family.

Lawson   Woah, honey. I didn't realise the world was spinning around you. You sound a little like your grandmother yourself. She thought she was pretty important as well.

Meena   I didn't mean to cause offence, maybe I should . . .

Ted   Maybe you should.

Lawson   You're going to disappear now? Never call?

Meena   I'm going to go.

Lawson   I was going to give you a ride to the airport but I don't know now I think we're busy – are we busy?

Ted   We're busy.

Meena   It's fine I'll go.

Lawson   Don't forget any of the shit you left lying around.

Meena   Look this hostility is / really not helping when all I'm trying to do is find out the facts! I'm just looking for the truth.

As **Meena** *speaks* **Jonathan** *has entered.*

Lawson   Hostility! Did you hear that, honey, in my own home! / I'm hostile! When she's the one, we've opened our doors and she's . . .

Ted   I think we should all calm down.

Jonathan   Did I hear something about waffles?

Ted   You did.

Jonathan   Great. Hey – did you get my email?

Ted (*sotto*)   Honey, I think we're all excited . . .

Meena   Your what?

Jonathan   Email.

Lawson (*sotto*)   I'll be less *excited* when she's out of my damn house, and you know you could be a little more *activated*.

Meena   Uh no, I haven't looked, I was just leaving.

Jonathan   No, stay.

Ted   If she wants to go she can go – (*To* **Lawson**.) She can go.

Lawson   Yeah.

Jonathan   No you have to stay.

A short small beat as everyone registers this as odd.

Jonathan   My mom . . . makes the best waffles.

Lawson   Thank you, honey.

Meena   I'm ok.

Jonathan   Yeah, you know, you're not one of us until you've had one of those waffles.

Meena   Sorry no I'm going, / thank you for having me.

Ted   Your mother's upset.

Jonathan   That sweet tooth, it's such a family thing isn't it, do you have that your / side? See –

Ted   Jonathan, leave it for right now, ok.

Jonathan   – I feel like I never even got to know you.

Ted   Jonathan, not right / this second.

Jonathan   It was so nice to meet you, Meena – Galway.

Pause.

Jonathan Right?

Meena What?

Jonathan Galway, right? Meena / Galway.

Lawson What's that, honey?

Jonathan Not Graham, Galway.

Meena Sorry, I don't [know what you mean].

Lawson Who's Galway?

Meena I think / there's been a confusion.

Jonathan I did a little research on our guest, and she's not who she says she is, she's not even family, she's been lying this whole time, she's a fucking fraud.

Ted What are you saying?		**Meena** Look I . . .	
	Lawson So who the hell are you?		
Woah, woah.	So who is she then?		**Jonathan** She's been recording everything we've been saying – you are not leaving until you give me that SD card.
Jonathan.		I . . . I . . .	
Jonathan, ok, Jonathan.	Jonny explain what you mean.	I'm sorry but.	Give me that SD card.
		I'm not going to give you that.	
Cool it, Jonathan!			Give me that SD card right now.

I haven't told
them

Told us what?

(*To* **Lawson**.)
Shut up and
let me deal
with this.

Excuse me!
Don't tell your
mother to shut
up!

(*To* **Ted**.) You
have no
fucking idea
what's
happening
right now ok.

Hey you do
not talk to
your father
like that.

No.

(*To* **Meena**.) Give me
that SD card.

What are you
even talking
about!

No absolutely
not.

Stop it!

Jonathan!

Give
me that SD
card you are
giving me that
SD card give
me that SD
card give me
(*lunging*) that
SD card now.
(*Shoves* **Ted**
back.) Get off
me! Don't
touch me!

(*Grabs* **Jonathan**
from lunging at
Meena.)

She exits.

Easy! Easy!
Ok!
What are you
so hyped up
about – I don't
give a shit
what's on that
recorder.

Jonathan   You don't get it! You don't fucking understand what's going on here!

Lawson   We got nothing to hide. Do you?

Radio static – a shift in time.

Jonathan   I have to! I've got twenty grand in student debt!

Ted   And nothing to / show for it.

Lawson   Is it illegal?

Jonathan   No / it's not, Mom . . .

Lawson   Can just anyone see these articles?

Jonathan   Mom, I'm not going to explain the internet to you.

Radio static – a shift in time.

Lawson Do not talk to your son like that – you're as bad as him.	**Jonathan** Fucking hell, Dad.

Ted (*to* **Lawson**)   You treat him like a baby – this is why he's like this, that's the problem. No no no no no that's why he's a grown man living with his parents and he can't finish school . . .

(*To* **Ted**.) Oh so this is my fault? If you'd like to take part in raising our child then please! Door's open!

Go fuck yourself ok, you fucking asshole – you can both go fuck yourselves. I'm the only one here . . .

Radio static – a shift in time.

Ted   Leave!
Go!
Let him go!

Jonathan   Can't
fucking stand it!
I'm out! I'm
fucking out!

Lawson (*to*
Jonathan)   Ok if
that's what you
want to do then
fine, you go ahead,
but that's it, and
you better be
ready for what
comes after.
Believe me.

Radio static – a shift in time.

Margaret (*very upset*)   You left me. (*Beat*) You didn't even
look for me. (*Beat*) You took Eddie and left me behind. You
saved Eddie. But you left me to . . . to . . . left me to . . .

Ma (*as kind as possible*)   Margaret, honey. That's not what
happened.

Radio static – a shift in time.

Ma   The kids, the
kids. (*To* **Edward**.)
Edward, come
here. (*To* **Pa**.) Get
Margaret,
Edward. Edward.
Where's your
sister? Have you
seen your sister?
Where is she? Ok,
honey, it's ok –
Margaret! Don't
hide now come
out! (*To* **Pa**.) She

Edward   What's
the noise?

I don't know.

No.

Where's
Margaret?

Pa   Margaret!
Margaret!
She's not there,
she's next door I
saw her – I think I
saw her . . . [leave]
She's not here,
she's next door –
come on.
We've got to go.

hides sometimes!   What's
She might be   happening?
hiding – check
everywhere!   She's not here – I
                                               have! We've got to
                                               go *now*!

Radio static – a shift in time.

Pa   Margaret! Margaret! Margaret! Margaret!

Ma (*entering*)   Nothing?

Pa   Nothing – you?

Ma   Can't find her anywhere.

Pa   Think she's with that new pal of hers?

Edward (*entering*)   She's not next door and Mikey says he hasn't seen her since lunch.

Ma   Think we should call the police?

Pa   I don't know.

Radio static – a shift in time.

Ma   I'm just
not so sure! I
think we need
to think about
this rationally   **Pa**   There isn't   **Margaret**
and calmly.   time to think!   Sounds pretty
I don't want us   This is   real to me.
wrecking the   happening
house if . . .   now!

                                   Edward   It's
                                   not on any
                                   other station.

                      Because   Just to be safe
                      they've stopped   though!
                      broadcasting!   Don't
But aliens,   They don't   you want to
sweetheart, I   want panic!   just in case?

just don't think
. . .

> Of course not,
> it's the
> Germans, they
> mean the
> Germans.

But maybe
that's wrong
but the rest of
it's true.

Radio static – a shift in time.

Ma *comforts* **Edward** *as* **Pa** *and* **Margaret** *talk.*

Pa (*steamrolling*)
What you have to
understand is that
there wasn't time
to make a decision,
we only had time
for action, and we
had to get going
or risk our own
lives and when
you didn't come
when we called we
thought you were
off somewhere
and we thought,
we hoped we'd
find you on the
way.

Margaret I can't
listen to this –
however you slice
it you still left me
and it doesn't
matter if it was
real or not. Ma,
you cannot just
leave me when
you thought – I
can't do this, I
can't take any
more of this, I'm
out, I'm out of
here – (*Exiting.*) I
wish you *had* been
vaporised by
Martians!

Ma It wasn't real,
honey, so how
about we forget all
this.

Out where now?
Don't do . . .

Edward (*running out after her*) Madge!

Radio static – a shift in time.

Orson This is what I was trying to say! With my work!
My art!

Orson I wanted to wake you up. Everything that came out
of this new magic box was believed.

Orson Consumed without question.

Orson   I had to do something, something.

Orson   This is what I was trying to tell you! But you weren't listening!

Orson   I wanted you to learn from this. You can't swallow everything that comes through the tap.

Orson *holds out the microphone – now bearing the logo of a UK news broadcaster.*

Orson   You learned the wrong lesson.

As the **Announcer** *speaks, the three remaining company each look into the light coming from their palms – a smartphone.*

Announcer   We are unable to continue our broadcast from Grovers Mill, Evidently there's some difficulty with our field transmission. However, we will return you at the earliest opportunity. Latest update, tragically the body of Carl Phillips has been identified in a Trenton hospital. National Red Cross reports ten units of Red Cross emergency workers have been assigned to the headquarters of the state militia, and the fires at Grovers Mill and vicinity are now under control. However under martial law no one will be permitted to enter this area except by special pass issued by state or military authorities. Four companies of state militia are proceeding from Trenton to Grovers Mill, and will aid in the evacuation of homes within the range of military operations. I'm just getting a message in . . . Yes we have a connection with General Lansing who is on site with the shell that landed earlier in Worthing. General Lansing, can you hear me?

General Lansing *– like all the reporting characters – is lit by the palm lights.*

Lansing   Yes this is General Lansing on site.

Announcer   Thank you for finding time to speak to us today. Can you tell us a bit about what's going on, what you can see?

Lansing   Yes I can. The cylindrical object which lies in a pit directly below our position is surrounded on all sides – the situation is now under complete control.

Something to the side has arrested **General Lansing***'s attention.*

Announcer   That is good to hear – how do you expect this to proceed from here?

Lansing   Uh . . .

Announcer   General?

Lansing   I'm sorry you're going to have to repeat that.

Announcer   Can you clarify what you can see?

Lansing   Kind of shield-like appears to be rising up.

Transmission cuts out.

Announcer   General Lansing? General Lansing can you hear us? Ok, we seem to have lost our signal with General Lansing but I'm sure we'll reconnect as soon as possible. In the meantime we take you to our reporter in the field Richard Sander who is nearby. Richard, what is the situation where you are?

Richard *just waits to be put through.*

Announcer   Richard, can you hear me? / Richard, we can hear you. Richard?

Richard (*off mic*)   Are we there? I'm not hearing her, not hearing anything. No, nothing.

Announcer   Ok, we'll come back to Richard later. Right now we have I think an eyewitness on the line for us, Christina Sutton. Christina can you hear me?

Christina   Hello, yeah, I can.

Announcer   Great. Christina, you're local to the area, can you tell me about what's been happening this evening?

Christina   Yeah, it's been such a weird evening to be honest with you I don't really know what's going on to be honest, it's just a lot of chaos.

Announcer   Can you tell us what the scene is like there now, Christina?

Christina   Um, yeah, there's a lot of smoke and, um, a lot of noise and, I don't know to be honest, it's just a lot going on and, um, like earlier there was this green flash but I don't know what that is but now it's just a lot of smoke and noise / and yeah . . .

Announcer   Thank you, Christina – I think we've re-established our connection with Richard. Richard, can you hear me now?

Richard   Yes I can – apologies for earlier.

Announcer   That's not a problem, Richard, it sounds like there's quite a state of alarm there. We just spoke to an eyewitness near you – can you shed any light on what's happening over there?

Richard   Yes, we're being told that the threat level has been placed at severe and that people are being told to stay in their homes unless it's an absolute / emergency, that goes for . . .

Announcer   I'm sorry, I'm going to have to cut you off, Richard, we're going now to a live address –

Politician   I shall not try to conceal the gravity of the situation that confronts the country, nor the concern of your government in protecting the lives and property of its people. However, I wish to impress upon you the urgent need of calm and resourceful action. Fortunately, this formidable enemy is still confined to a comparatively small area, and we may place our faith in the military forces to keep them there. We must confront this destructive adversary with a nation united, courageous, and consecrated to the preservation of the human species on earth. I thank you.

Announcer   You have just heard the – uh, a new report coming in. Ok, gosh, I have a grave announcement to make. (*Reading from the prompter.*) Incredible as it may seem, both the observations of science and the evidence of our eyes lead to the inescapable assumption that those strange beings who landed this evening are the vanguard of an invading army from the planet Mars. Here are – there are too many bulletins to read here. Ok, yes, we have a live – no, we're going to – uh, I uh . . . I don't really know. (*To the unseen studio director.*) Which am I reading? . . . Berlin . . . sorry, sorry . . .

The **Announcer** *takes their mic away and talks to the studio director as the sound around them builds.*

Announcer (*less audible*)   You need to cut to national, I need to get my kids – no I'm getting my kids I'm not staying, cut to national – let someone else do it!

The **Announcer** *goes to exit but stops themselves, turns back – now* **Orson***, they look out at the audience as they sweep their arms up, cueing chaos.*

The lights go out, sirens and cacophony burst into the space, emergency lights flicker and searchlights spin, as the actors reset the stage . . .

Lights up on the original radio studio – the mic has CBS facing out again.

One actor speaks as **Orson** *gently guides them through their monologue and orchestrates the sounds around their speech.*

The other actors watch.

Actor   I'm speaking from the roof of the Broadcasting Building, New York City. The bells you hear are ringing to warn the people to evacuate the city as the Martians approach. Estimated in last two hours three million people

have moved out along the roads to the north, Hutchison
River Parkway still kept open for traffic. Avoid bridges to
Long Island . . . hopelessly jammed. All communication with
Jersey shore closed ten minutes ago. No more defences. Our
army wiped out . . . artillery, air force, everything wiped out.
This may be the last broadcast. I'll stay here to the end . . .
people are holding service below us . . . in the cathedral.
Streets are all jammed. Enemy now in sight above the
Palisades. Five – five great machines. First one is crossing
river. I can see it from here, wading the Hudson like a man
wading through a brook . Now the first machine reaches the
shore. Stands watching. The steel, cowlish head is even with
the skyscrapers. It waits for the others. They rise like a line
of new towers on the city's west side . . . now they're lifting
their metal hands. This is the end now. Smoke comes out . . .
black smoke, drifting over the city. People in the streets see it
now. They're running towards the East River . . . thousands
of them, dropping in like rats. Now the smoke's spreading
faster. It's reached Times Square. People trying to run away
from it, but it's no use. They're falling like flies.

Announcer   You have been listening to a CBS presentation
of Orson Welles and the Mercury Theatre on the air in an
original dramatisation of The War of the Worlds by H.G.
Wells.

Orson   Of course you would have.

Orson   Every single one of you.

Orson   It's not my fault if a thirteen-year-old girl – if a
family – if everyone believes it.

Orson   You want to believe.

Blackout.

Skype call tone.

A harsh spotlight up on **Nick** *on one far side of the stage, at a
microphone, facing the audience.*

Nick　Hello? Hello?

Lawson (*still in the dark, speaking through a microphone*)　Hello?

Nick　Hello?

A harsh spotlight up on **Lawson** *on the other far side of the stage, at a microphone, facing the audience.*

Lawson *and* **Nick** (*happy that it's now working*)　Ah!

Nick　How's that?

Lawson　Yes, so much better!

Nick　Alright, good. I tend to find this easier.

Lawson　Thank you for showing me how to do it – I'm going to use it to call my son – he's going to hate it.

Nick (*laughs, beat*)　So.

Lawson　So, this is a, a hoot.

Nick　Yes it is.

Lawson　Never thought you'd be having this conversation I bet. Hey, how tall are you?

Nick　Six foot.

Lawson　Oh my goodness.

Nick　My father was tall.

Lawson　That's where it is then because I am not six foot!**

They laugh.

** *If the actor playing* **Lawson** *is not significantly shorter than* **Nick**, *then the following dialogue can be used instead:*

Lawson　Never thought you'd be having this conversation I bet. Hey, how tall are you?

Nick　Six foot.

Lawson　You see, I should have known. You look much more like a Kavakas than Meena did.

Lawson   But you do look more like a Kavakas than Meena did!

Nick   I want to just apologise again, / when she said she wanted to interview me –

Lawson   Oh no don't, please.

Nick   – I really had no idea . . .

Lawson   How were you to know?

Nick   You've been so nice / about it –

Lawson   I wasn't at first!

Nick   – but you know if it was me and someone was invading my family / my home – I'm furious.

Lawson   Oh hush, no, I welcomed her in. I mean I thought she was related at the time sure, cousin or second cousin or something, but she was a nice girl. Kinda wish she was my cousin. Maybe that's why I was so quick to trust – wish I had more family in general I think.

Nick   Me too actually.

Lawson   Yeah?

Nick   Yeah. My husband / has a large family.

Lawson   Your husband?

Nick   Yes.

Lawson   Ok. Great, your *husband*, sorry for barging in there, ok your husband . . .?

Nick   He just has a very large family. We normally go to theirs for events like Christmas and Easter even. And it's really nice, and I do sometimes think: what would it have been like if I'd had that? If they'd just . . . said what was needed to be . . . I did try to get Mum to contact you.

Lawson   You did?

Nick   Yeah but she was, she wanted to let sleeping dogs lie. And I didn't know . . . and I didn't feel able . . .

Lawson   Well, it's hard to know what to do isn't it. When you don't know what really, what's really going on.

Nick   Right.

Lawson   So you're going to theirs this year? For Christmas?

Nick   Yes. Same as always. What are your Christmas plans?

Lawson   Oh, we never have very big ones – you know, go to church. Our son was living with us but now he's moved out. To LA! He's in LA now, my God. It's great for him – this presidency is good for some of us it seems, some Facebook TV thing out there, some viral thing, I don't understand it but he's happy. We voted for Hillary by the way, so you know, we agreed we were voting for Hillary, that was what we agreed, me and Ted. I can only speak for myself, but, anyway . . . Christmas is going to be different this year. Where are your husband's family?

Nick   They're in the Peak District.

Lawson   The Peak District. Ok, is that near London?

Nick   No, quite far actually.

Lawson   What, five hours?

Nick   Oh no, no, three.

Lawson   Oh that's near! Try New Jersey to LA!

Nick   I forget that England is so much smaller / than the States.

Lawson   I know, it's a wonder anything gets done really, so many people. And no wonder we have more crazies, there's just more of us in general!

Nick   We have our fair share, trust me. Maybe not so direct, but they're definitely there.

Lawson   I guess in England you're all so close you bump up against crazies more, right? Like in New York?

Nick   That is what London is like, actually.

Lawson   Still I'd love to go to London, ah, love to.

Nick   You should visit.

Lawson   Visit you?

Nick   Yes, visit us.

Lawson   Do you mean that?

Nick   Of course I do. We'll split the cost / of course.

Lawson   Oh no, no, no.

Nick   No, no, I want to, / it would be nice.

Lawson   Oh that is so, just so . . . (*Turning away from her microphone.*) Can I say something?

Spotlights dissolve as house lights come up.

Nick *is caught off-guard, stays close to his mic, surprised and unsure.*

Nick   Uh, yes?

Lawson   I was so scared.

Nick (*leaving his microphone*)   You were scared?

Lawson   So scared to talk to you, but you're a very nice person. And, you know, my father's sister, your mom, I only ever heard it from my father's point of view. And you're wonderful, so I think, she must have been a little wonderful too.

Nick   She was . . . not perfect.

They smile.

Nick   But she did talk about the States a lot. I think in her way she was saying something similar.

They embrace.

A recording studio.

Paolo It really is so affecting. We're just all very excited to start work on it.

Meena So before we, can I, um, I need to . . .

Paolo Everything alright?

Meena Yeah, I'm fine, I just feel . . . can I speak to you a second?

Paolo Of course – (*To the tech desk.*) Let's take a smoker's break, guys.

The **Technicians** *leave on break.*

Paolo (*to* **Meena**) You don't have to get it right first time –

Meena No, I, um . . .

Paolo – it's best just to get the jitters out in the recording, you know, dive in, and we can do a couple of options and see what works.

Meena It's not really that, it's, I . . . I'm just wondering if we can do this some other way?

Paolo The set-up?

Meena The story. I'm just thinking, I'm just having second thoughts.

Paolo Ah.

Meena Because you know, what if . . . because I lied.

Paolo You let me worry about that. We can deal with that, we've done it before. You're not going to go to *prison*. (*Laughs a little.*) We have a whole team to deal with that. You just worry about (*pointing to the mic*) this.

Meena But no I'm also, that's also what I'm worried about.

Paolo Ok?

Meena   I'm just worried – because I knew her.

Paolo   Right.

Meena   And when it was just an interview with Nick that's – but he's withdrawn his consent now / –

Paolo   Ok, so consent . . .

Meena   – and I just feel really weird because not only now has Nick said / he doesn't want to –

Paolo   Let's calm down.

Meena   – but the family doesn't even / know I'm doing it and this is all –

Paolo   Relax.

Meena   – it's really fantastic being here, working with you, that's really a dream, really a dream, but at what cost? You know? I don't know. I don't want to . . . I don't want to.

Paolo   You don't want to what?

Meena   I don't want to, betray . . . betray . . .

Paolo   Betray what? Sorry, hold on – he said this, right? He did this, you saw it. You talked to him about it.

Meena   Yeah.

Paolo   So it's all already out there. We're just turning on the lights. You're just being a reporter.

Meena   But he's taken it down now . . .

Paolo   He's been 'betraying' his readership the whole time he's been doing this.

Meena   He's just young though.

Paolo   He gave us Trump!

Meena   Not *him*.

Paolo   People like him! Don't kid yourself. You don't feel sorry for *him* do you? (*Beat.*) Because we can go lighter on the dead mother stuff, fine, if that'll sort out Nick for you, that's not the story. Look, I've got to be honest with you. This is something really special. So current. This is exactly what listeners are looking for right now. They're hungry for it. And you've got an opportunity . . . It's going to be a zeitgeist moment. And I admire your ethics, I do, but you're acting like this is your story when it's not. It doesn't belong to you, it belongs to all of us, because all of us are living with the consequences of this sort of – you want my personal opinion? My personal, unprofessional opinion? My very unprofessional opinion is: fuck him. He's only getting what's coming to him. Fuck all of them. You want to cut him slack because he's young? He's an adult. He knew what he was doing, I wasn't doing this at his age, and you're not far apart – would you do what he did? And if you don't tell people what he did, aren't you complicit? Meena, you need to make this. You have a responsibility. (*Shift in tone.*) But. It's your podcast, your decision.

Pause as **Meena** *considers.*

The **Technicians** *et al. have started to return and watch from the booth, waiting to see if they're needed.*

Paolo (*softer*)   How about we just make a start. And if at any point you want to stop everything, you can stop everything. And you and I can just . . . keep in touch. (*Beat – he holds the script out to her.*) Have a crack at the start. See how it feels. See how it sounds.

Meena *takes the script and her position behind the mic.*

Paolo *gives a signal to the* **Technicians**.

Meena *stands at the microphone, reads and thinks.*

She struggles.

She swallows her nerves.

She speaks, unsure at first, then building confidence.

As she speaks, the sound world of the podcast builds around her.

Meena   A . . . (*clears throat*) a country, built on a story. A democracy, broken by falsehoods. A president, elected through fear. A referendum, won on confusion. A town, identified by a fiction. A family, split by lies. And a son, at the centre of it all, remaking the world from his childhood bedroom.

Jonathan (*V/O*)   *It's my job to give these people what they want and guess what they want –*

Meena   I'm Meena Galway.

End.

For a complete listing of Bloomsbury
Methuen Drama titles, visit:
www.bloomsbury.com/drama

Follow us on Twitter and keep up to date
with our news and publications

@MethuenDrama